A FOWLER'S WORLD

A FOWLER'S WORLD

*Recollections of Wildfowling
on Marsh and Estuary*

IAN NIALL

with illustrations by

C.F. TUNNICLIFFE

Foreword by

BERNARD O'DONOGHUE

White Lion Books

CAMBRIDGE

White Lion Books
An imprint of
Colt Books Ltd
9 Clarendon Road
Cambridge CB2 2BH
Tel: (0223) 357047 Fax: (0223) 65866

This new edition first published by White Lion Books 1994

First published in 1968 by William Heineman Ltd

Text © Ian Niall 1968
Illustrations © Estate of C.F. Tunnicliffe 1994
Introduction © Bernard O'Donoghue 1994

ISBN 1 874762 06 6

British Library Cataloguing-in-Publication Data
A catalogue record for this book is available from the British Library

Design by Clare Byatt

Printed in Great Britain by Biddles Ltd, Guildford.

CONTENTS

For my friend Selwyn Roderick

IAN NIALL is the author of eleven novels and many books on country matters including *Pastures New* and *Fresh Woods*. In 1990 he celebrated forty years as a columnist, beginning with *The Spectator* and then *Country Life*, where he is known and loved by a wide public for his regular contributions to 'A Countryman's Notes'. He was born in Scotland and he spent his formative years on his grandfather's farm in Wigtownshire, recalled in *A Galloway Childhood*. Married with three grown up children and five grandchildren, he and his wife now live in the Chilterns after more than forty years in Wales.

CHARLES TUNNICLIFFE (1901–1979) was raised on a small farm in Cheshire. He was expected to take over his father's smallholding, but his precocious talent as an artist set him apart and in 1920 he took a scholarship to the Royal College of Art. Tunnicliffe soon made his mark as an etcher and wood-engraver and in 1932 came his first major success with his illustrated edition of *Tarka the Otter* by Henry Williamson. He went on to illustrate dozens of books for well-known authors. He also produced several classic books of his own including his masterpiece *Shorelands Summer Diary*. Had Tunnicliffe done nothing other than illustrate books, his name would be remembered. But his achievement as a wildlife artist, and in particular as a bird artist, is of major importance. Turning to the study of birds in the 1930s, he spent long hours observing and sketching his favourite species, first on the Cheshire meres and nearby moors, then in Anglesey, his home from 1947 until his death in 1979.

BERNARD O'DONOGHUE was born in Cullen in the rural depths of North Cork in 1945. He moved to Manchester in 1962 and since 1965 he has lived in Oxford where he teaches English at Magdalen College. He has written on medieval English, as well as four books of poetry: *Razorblades and Pencils* (1984); *Poaching Rights* (1987); *The Absent Signifier* (1990); *The Weakness* (1991). His wife Heather is a scholar of Old Norse; they have three children.

AUTHOR'S NOTE

What follows is a picture of a personal world
rather than of the wildfowler's world in general.
It contains no more than experience and is not
intended to be a guide to anyone but the uncom-
mitted novice in the hope that he may come to
appreciate my world in which impressions and
atmosphere are more important than getting a
duck or a goose for dinner.

FOREWORD
by Bernard O'Donoghue

I remember a wet Sunday afternoon in my childhood when my father was mocked for returning empty-handed from a rare shooting expedition. He explained that he had got near to shooting a cock pheasant but, by the time he had satisfied himself that it was not a hen, it was out of range.

I had entirely forgotten this small event until reading *A Fowler's World*. I expect that the book's elegant evocativeness will prompt every reader's memory in one way or another. Nor is it accidental that it is an act of humane responsibleness that the book recalled. Ian Niall is a good fowler who gives shrewd advice on how to set about shooting; but he is just as much a storyteller and naturalist: one of his most delightful books is *Feathered Friends*. At times even in *A Fowler's World* the naturalist's interests take precedence, as when he describes the 'trance' that goose behaviour induces, holding back the trigger:

> I am no longer a novice. It is more than nerves that stops me, a sort of amazement. There is no time to shoot when I stand and see the pinions of the goose waving, the tucked-up feet, the outstretched necks, the barred bellies, the soft grey and white feathers.

Elsewhere Niall tells of a snowy day from his childhood when his family let a flock of greylag geese fly past the front of the house unmolested, attributing the truce to the fact that the 'poor things had wandered, lost like wethers out on the hill'.

So if you start this book expecting to find a kind of ruthless Papageno you will be disappointed; the birdcatcher's methods, indeed, are said to be 'much more brutal than the blunderbuss'.

What you get is something more like the elegiac Yeats of 'The Wild Swans at Coole'. Niall ponders the crowding seashore wigeon:

> Where were they before they began to gather in the estuary in October? Where did they nest and how did they come? Where will they go when they take their leave in late February or March?

Where indeed! Yeats's famous *ubi sunt* inevitably comes to mind:

> Among what rushes will they build,
> By what lake's edge or pool
> Delight men's eyes when I awake some day
> To find they have flown away?

Not, of course, that Niall is not serious about the skills of the fowler's trade. What his elegy is largely about is the passing of the world in which those skills could be effectively plied. 'Nowhere in Britain remains remote,' he laments; the essential solitude of the fowler has gone. And, if for much of the time the geese themselves are the heroes of this book (their passing overhead is celebrated again and again, at one point causing old men to 'look up as though assured of eternal life'), they have to divide the writer's admiration with the dedicated, friendless, one-armed fowler of the last chapter, 'Odd Birds'. What becomes more pronounced throughout the book is the insistence that the fowler and his quarry are in it together, as that last chapter's title makes clear. The second-last chapter, 'Ancient Art', is concerned with decoy-making, identifying the lure which traps alike the duck and the decoy-maker as the same instinctive obsession. It is all a matter of natural selection. And most of the time the duck and goose are the better equipped artists in this exterior world.

At one point Niall issues a challenge to his artistic illustrator to capture this world, recalling 'the old print quality' of the moonlit countryside as it appeared in some Russian tinted engravings he remembers. C.F. Tunnicliffe has responded magnificently – and typically – to the challenge in his line-engravings of the tidal shore or the moon behind saplings. The few strokes with which he can fill the sky and the page with birds is reminiscent of the pointillism of Louis le Brocquy. Best of all is his one-armed dedicated fowler amongst the 'Odd Birds'. He is the perfect representer of Niall's world in which, as he tells us in his Author's Note, 'impressions and atmosphere are more important than getting a duck or a goose for dinner'. Like Walton's *Compleat Angler*, this is a book about hunting; but, also like Walton, by attending to its subject with devotion it comes to be about much more than that. It is a book of wisdom.

BERNARD O' DONOGHUE
Oxford 1994

Waterbirds

WHATEVER use the arable land of this country is put to, whether it is whittled away by developers or land-greedy builders, or its acreage increased by reclaimed land from its fringes, there will always be many thousands of acres of wilderness, marsh, bog, and swamp beyond reclaim. By the nature of things there is a balance which the engineer's bravest efforts can hardly influence. Land is recovered here and eroded there, but apart from this there is a timeless wilderness that had no recorded beginning and will remain as the tide ebbs and flows. In all these wild places there are waterbirds of one sort or another, birds that lived in the quiet parts of the swamp and the mud of the estuary when monsters wallowed there and men lived in caves. The waterbird attracts the bird-watcher, the photographer, the naturalist, but the fowler has haunted the marshes longer than any other sort of man.

Everyone who is drawn to the haunts of waterbirds carries away with him something intangible. There is more than the eye sees, a sort of poetry, a music that lingers. The colour of this world isn't always strong. It may be in the delicate coming of the dawn, the burst of sunrise, the quenching of the sun when it sets on the widest possible horizon, with waterbirds dotting a sand that is like a mirror of the brilliant sky, or it may be the green on the head of a mallard drake, the blue-and-white brand on the wing. The music is like the music of a great orchestra, something that remains in the mind after the performance is finished. Solos are played in flute tones by individual birds that have a phrase or two to contribute. There are wonderful instruments played by unseen players, instruments that have the strange sound of Eastern music, because the coot, the duck, the bittern, waders of one sort or another, have minor roles as well as major ones, sometimes marking the chords with singular emphasis and sometimes trilling. Long afterwards the listener hears this concert, a concert of muted notes and strident calling, aggressive drakes, joyful geese, testing the echoes of the very dome of the sky above. All this is part of the substance of a fowler's enjoyment, something he discovers and delights in without ever pausing to examine the constituent parts of his enjoyment, this and the primeval attraction of secret places, pools, drains, waterholes, lonely lochs and creeks. It is a recollection of visual things at the same time, a subconscious recording of the clear water-rolling sand in the current, the sculpting of mud by the wash of the tide.

In such places as these I have been blissfully happy. It began so long ago that I can hardly say exactly when I began to study the fowl that are the proper study of a fowler—mallard, teal, wigeon, pinkfeet geese, greylags and white-fronted, black geese, and the big, honking Canada goose which has spread these few years back from private ponds and lakes but will never, as far as I can see, compete with any of the greys. The lesser fowl are just as fascinating as the sort that fly in majestic formation and follow each other in echelons so high in the heavens that few men can resist the temptation to stand and stare. But the lesser fowl man puts on his plate are few in number. They include the snipe and woodcock, although the woodcock is listed as game, the curlew, whimbrel, plovers golden and grey, redshank, bar-tailed godwit, eaten by fowlers who hunt for sport and table. This is a world of escape, of course, a world for the dreamer. Some people imply that a man must be ashamed of dreaming. The same people would regulate all private thoughts and reproach those who would slip their collar and harness for a day or two. They are the builders of the concrete world. Their music is the ticking of the busy clock, the clicking of the computer. The glow of neon warning-lights colours their world.

The world in which I would have you travel has something that so far has survived the destruction of empires and the crumbling of cities. In his heart every man knows it is the natural world to which he really belongs.

If there was a beginning, it was down along the burnside where the waterhen nested. I have a habit of going back on things to examine carefully how my enjoyment of them began. The waterhens of the burn were there on the field below the hill on which I first saw a hare snared and on the very pasture where I set a snare myself. I discovered that the waterhens had nested on the burn before I was born because people who never went to look at them knew they were there and were part of the world in which we lived. They had always been there and although many things have changed since my childhood I am willing to wager that so long as that burn runs from the back moss down through the same fields, under the same cart bridges, and between the same patches of round rushes,

waterhens will still be found there. It would impair my
picture of life to think that it could be otherwise. I found
the waterhens going helterskelter across the field when I
followed our domestic ducks down to the water where
they paddled and flapped and stretched their wings and
quacked. The duck sometimes laid their eggs in the duck
house and the eggs were lost in the mud on the floor, but
often they dropped an egg in the burn itself. If we went
down there before the slow flow of the peaty, stout-
coloured water coated the sunken eggs with a black covering of peat they could be retrieved. With the excuse of
going to see if there were any duck eggs to be salvaged
I was allowed to visit the burn, except when it was in
spate. The waterhens became my every-day study and a
source of continual fascination. They were birds that lived
secretively and came and went unobtrusively as the mallard
flies in the dusk or in the morning. The burn, draining
the hollow where the potatoes grew, ran from the corner
of the low planting, where it was only a trickle of water
among the stones, through high banks of fern and walls
of bracken, under a railway sleeper bridge, and past tall,
unkempt hawthorn trees, rusty wire fences, a dozen
drinking-places and the nests of yellow-hammers, hedge-
sparrows, long-tailed tits in the gorse, partridges on the
banks. In its course there were trout here and there, and
jerking, wriggling freshwater shrimps, leeches, elvers,
watersnails, water-beetles as well as skaters, those incredibly light creatures which race across the surface of a pool
and find hiding-places among the plants that grow
between the stones.

Generations of boys had come down from the old steading, as I came down, to explore the burnside and find the
waterhen's nest, and still the birds frequented the place,
belonging like the barn owl in the chimney of the house,
the swallows in the cartshed. It takes wilful intent to
destroy such regularity of habit. Waterbirds, like the fish

in a stream, will live where they can get food and the opportunity to breed. The waterhen's nest was robbed, but only of a limited number of eggs. It was never damaged and some eggs always hatched. I was guilty of taking eggs. A girl picks a flower; a boy takes an egg, until he knows better. Worse things are done by grown men who already know better. I had waterhen eggs for my breakfast, but the bird had to be left with four eggs. My indiscrimate milking of the eggs as they were laid must have ensured that in the end I would eat one that was partly incubated, or at least far from fresh. I grew a little older. The waterhens taught me a lot about the elusiveness of wildfowl.

Although the pursuit of the waterhen hardly ranks as wildfowling, it was this that set the course of my apprenticeship. I would have gone after the wild geese or the mallard that sometimes came across the fields, but my stride was short and my means of doing so more than slightly limited. If my thoughts were with the hurrying duck, when I came back to earth I would see the tracks of the waterhen on the expanse of black peat left by the shrinking water of the burn. I studied the signs and was fascinated by the feathers I sometimes found floating on the water or blown into the grass. I could spend hours in the scent of water-plants. I loved the fragrance of fern and the heavy perfume of the blossom when the hawthorn flourished. I discovered the secret of the waterhen's world and how they travelled up and down the burn, elusive as the corncrake in the long grass at times, furtive like the rarer water rail, slipping across banks of mud the way a bank-vole moves, diving and swimming with such grace that to see them underwater was breathtaking. Sometimes I only knew I had seen them after they had gone from sight. Sometimes I watched for them to break cover and almost run along the top of the water as they crossed a place that was wide and shallow. It was a futile exercise by adult standards, I suppose, but my time was a child's time, marked by very few significant chimes of the clock.

There came a change in all this, however. I suppose I really began to hunt and ceased to be innocent when Willie came on the scene. Willie was one of my grand-father's labourers. I think he was the most idle and the most irresponsible of the men the old man employed. He was certainly the most hungry for he could eat anything, anywhere and at any time. He loved to dig up the bulbous root of a grass which he said was a fairy potato, and he was equally partial to peas from the garden, blackberries, wild raspberries, and the eggs of lay-away hens quickly broken into his gaping mouth. But he was no vegetarian and would use the old gun with which he had been entrusted as the scarecrow of the place to get himself rabbits, or anything else he could cook. When I think of it now I am sure Willie was either a compulsive eater or host to an outsized tapeworm. It was certainly his prin-ciple aim in life to keep his hungry belly filled. He would quarter a field to rob the green plover in March and April, and search just as diligently for the nests of game-birds later on. One day, I recall, we had had duck for dinner and Willie, licking his lips after the feast, stood on the bridge of the cart road and looked at the waterhens out on the field. He decided there and then that we would have a hunt and he would have a between-meals snack of roasted waterhen. I am ashamed to say that I allowed myself to be recruited. But I had the knowledge of the escape routes of the birds. I was the ideal choice of a beater, one who knew every secret corner in the burn's course.

The waterhens had run into the burnside when we came down with the gun. Willie took his stand on a grassy mound beside a gorse bush that hung over the water. I was sent to bring the burn down, as it might be called. The plan worked well. I went all the way up the hollow to the railway sleeper bridge and came down, pausing in all the hiding-places of the birds, watching them slipping out of one bit of cover to the next, and making sure they didn't slip back past me. In the meantime Willie stood guard, the hammer of the gun cocked, his clumsy finger on the trigger, his gastric juices running freely. I knew where the birds had to show themselves. I knew where they would be back in the water again before Willie saw them. There was a minute or two when I didn't want to see them shot, and then I weakened and thought how Willie would reproach or even browbeat me for being so slow and stupid. I called to him when they were about to cross a patch of water at which they had newly arrived and he was ready when the second one flapped away, turning from the burn to try to cut a corner and get back under the safety of the bank. Willie was no great shot, but a waterhen lacks speed. He tumbled the bird. A minute or two later its long, thin body was dangling from his hand.

'Up to the stoneheap at the corner of the planting,' said Willie, 'and we'll soon have him plucked and roasted!'

I followed at his heels and helped collect gorse branches for a fire, but the waterhen should have been skinned. The down wouldn't be singed. It adhered like black, scorched wool on the carcass. The skin had a bitter taste. Willie's appetite died abruptly. He threw the blackened waterhen away over the drystone wall.

It was a long time before I shot a waterhen and made soup from it, which is about the only thing anyone can do with this species of fowl. It makes soup. The flesh has hardly any taste but a flavour of mud. The down cannot be plucked, or rubbed away, after it has been burned, without a great deal of trouble. The skin simply must be peeled off, for it is bitter. Willie, who had offended against so many of my grandfather's laws that his life was intolerable, packed his bag and marched away. I cannot remember his face now, although I have a recollection of a

gangling youth with a gun in his hands, waiting for the
waterhens that were mine, and afterwards holding the
dead bird in the air.

This was my first shooting expedition in the haunts of
waterbirds. It is hard to explain the excitement I experienced in such places when I encountered fowl of different
sorts, a mallard, for instance, on the well-weathered coil
of hay abandoned by the haymakers after weeks of rain;
a snipe intent upon its own affairs, walking the gutters of
the cart track and feeding where a snipe had hardly ever
been seen; a greylag goose all alone on the grass field,
pretending, it seemed to me, to be a domestic goose, and
once a scoter duck, far from its normal haunts, taking
flight from our great round rush bog in which there
always seemed to be something new and unusual to be
discovered.

It was a long time before I was allowed to venture in
such places and stay away until the flighting time. In the
beginning I was restricted to the home acres, which meant
that I might go out on a bright afternoon and try to come
up with the freshly arrived flight of golden plovers, or
stalk the curlews that came in twos or threes to the hay-
fields after they had all been raked. The curlews were a
challenge and my stalking provided amusement because
no matter what I did I rarely got within shooting distance
of these incredibly wary birds that cried so plaintively
and tantalized me as they slid away over the drystone
walls. The curlew, like the mallard, seeks the seclusion of
remote and quiet places in which to breed. Like the
summer duck, it haunts the fields when men have put
away their guns and are occupied with cultivation and
harvesting. But the curlew wasn't protected; it wasn't
particularly loved either, for in the country of my childhood legends were preserved and old wrongs discussed
whenever old men talked. The curlew had betrayed some
of our ancestors to the dragoons of Bloody Cumberland.

It was a cursed bird, they said, to be punished for its treachery as long as the persecution was remembered. I had to learn how to come up with the curlew.

Even a curlew isn't always alert and able to sweep to safety on every occasion, but, for a while, it seemed to me that they had something more than ordinary cunning. Perhaps the old people were right and they were charmed in some way? I had to learn that wildfowl, even as un-glamorous a fowl as the long-nebbed curlew, should be stalked with the aid of the wind and in the sound of the rain. These elements cover two of the warnings that birds which feed and rest on the ground depend upon: sound carried by the air, and, transmitting through the ground, the vibration of a man's footsteps. An old fowler who had seen my efforts to come up with birds put his hand on my shoulder and told me a simple rule: to watch where the birds were feeding, come up wind to them so that the slightest warning would be carried away, and if possible, go out when there was a good downpour of rain. Not only would I flush waterbirds along the burn and duck from the rushes, but I would be able to stalk the curlew on the open field.

Old men often have a fear that all the hardship of acquiring the knowledge they have gained will come to nothing and are sometimes eager to see that the youngster begins with the advantage of their own years. After dis-covering that the curlew wasn't charmed I began to listen to the old men who went to the bay for geese and down to the river for duck. I began to stalk waterbirds of all kinds. I shot curlews and found them good to eat when they were from the green field and the pastures early in the season, muddy when they had been feeding on the estuary for weeks. The same applied, of course, to the mallard. There is nothing so unpleasant as the taste of the mud and grit of the riverbank in the flesh of a duck that has been roosting on the mud for a month. Even the

goose has to be doctored to make it fit for the table when
it has been kept from the fields and confined to the
estuary by severe weather. But duck and geese and small
fowl are the subject of my story. They were just the
beginning, those waterhens by the burn and the few fowl
that came to the place where I spent my childhood.

2

A Gun for a Goose

In his eagerness to set off to the estuary or through the alders and willows surrounding the marsh many an apprentice fowler often goes ill-armed to stalk the roosting geese or duck that climb up into the sky with startling rapidity. It befits the man who will ultimately learn the secrets of the marsh to tarry a while and enjoy something with as much romance and fascination as anything he will experience at dawn or dusk while waiting for the flight. There were devices before the gun, nets and snares, traps and decoys, and some of them were fashioned with a wonderful cunning which, when we look upon them now, makes us wonder that man has lost so much of it. But the gun has always had more than cunning. It has a special aura of death, a deadliness about it, that makes some men look at it as they look upon a snake and others grasp it with a boldness that is not always justified.

The guns of the old fowlers have for the most part

rusted and rotted away. They stood in corners gathering dust and cobwebs, their triggers fusing to the lock-plates, their barrels corroding with the residue of burnt powder, or hung on hooks in the shadows of black beams until some seeker of antiques came to lift them down. By that time one of these ancient tools of the trade would have a special patina of age and neglect particularly if no one had bothered to put a drop of gin on the locks—gin, it was thought, was better than any sort of oil. Generally it would turn out that no one had pulled the ramrod out or tried to until it warped in the securing rings that held it below the barrel and wouldn't come free. The fowler's gun had to be held straight to bring down a goose far out on the sand, swung to the trailing line of geese sailing over the wheat stubbles, and sometimes it would blow out a ramrod which, in his haste, the fowler had forgotten to remove when charging and priming his piece.

When I was a boy the old guns were already curiosities. No one had much use for them. They were shaky and heavy. Most of them had at least one broken hammer or had the stock reinforced with a binding of wire. Some had been modified in different ways to make them more usable when they had become worn. They had about them the line of fashion belonging to another century. Their stocks were often crude but sometimes slender and graceful: one might have an iron heel plate, another a trimming of inlaid brass or silver. Most were disfigured, dented, scarred, before they came to be discarded.

I remember when I discovered that geese and duck often fly higher and much farther out than expected. The range of a twelve-bore gun may be forty yards, but in the wilderness there is often very little that a fowler can use to check relative distance and I lacked the experience to compensate for this kind of drawback. I fired a few times and watched the fowl going on. It wasn't long before I concluded that the old heavy guns that the goose-shooters used were made as they were for something more than fad or fancy. It needed a strong back, a muscular shoulder, a certain determination, to put up such a heavy gun and take the recoil, but these old guns were made for the marsh where a man would perhaps get only one or two chances—after getting drenched with rain or hammered with hailstones—when the flight came.

I was daunted by the limitations of the conventional hammer gun I had been given and I made diligent search for old guns or bits of old guns that were said to be lying buried in corners of outbuildings or in old chests in lofts. I found the things they told me about; relics, the butt, or the broken stock of a flint-lock, the barrel of some sort of gun that had been crushed by the wheel of a cart or the dinner-plate hoof of a working-horse. I examined these things, turned them over in my hands, conscious that someone else, perhaps someone long dead, had carried the gun of which they were a part. I saw the old fowler stop to charge his gun, tipping his powder into the muzzle, tamping down his paper wad, measuring his shot and pouring it, firming everything in the barrel with a final stopper of paper, capping the nipple so that every-thing was ready for the shot. I saw the puff of smoke and the teal tumbling. Such a world was peaceful, populated only by men who hunted the marsh, walked the river, lay in hiding beside the waterhole; by fowlers and their dogs, shaggy water spaniels, lean and intelligent lurchers, retrievers, man and dog keeping each other company, lying close together to keep warm, watching the grey sky, breathing a steamy breath. The broken stock, the frac-tured hammer, the rusted nipple on the muzzle-loader that was hardly distinguishable from a piece of iron water-pipe, all set me day-dreaming. One day, I would come by a fowler's gun. Black powder could still be bought. If I found myself lacking shot I might use tintacks or chopped

nails, as my grandfather had done. I chose to forget that
the old man bore the scars of his folly. His gun had burst.
What of that? Had he not brought down more than his
share of birds before that happened?

There was a time when I almost laid hands on the gun
for the goose. I remember talking about it in the stable
and someone scratching his head and recalling that he
knew where such a gun was to be had. It stood, I was told,
at the back of an empty corn-chest in the unused stable
of a neighbouring farm. It had been there since the day
the farm had been tenanted. Our fields marched with the
boundary of this particular place, now taken in by another
neighbour, and no longer cultivated but used for wintering
bullocks and grazing for sheep. The farmhouse was
blind, its windows boarded up. The byre door hung on
broken hinges. Cattle and wandering donkeys went in and
out of the buildings as they pleased, sheltering from the
gales in winter and the flies in summer. The place had
the atmosphere of all derelict farms but if one stood in the
nettle-grown court or among the docks and ragwort of
the rickyard for a little while the past came to life. In
imagination one heard the voices of children, the squeal
of a pig, the crowing of cocks and the barking of the dog.
The chimney, blackened and moss-grown, seemed to trail
a wisp of smoke. Inside the shuttered house a caged bird
sang.

I had been in the stable many times. I hadn't seen the
gun that was supposed to be there, the fowler's gun with
the long, heavy barrel and the hammer like a rampant
horse, but I had only to think of it and I knew it was there.
I could see it. I could hardly wait to go haring over our
fields, across the drystone wall that was our march and
on through the wet moss, thorns and brambles that
crowded the sheep tracks on the way to the deserted
steading. I had company. Willie had a wonderful optimism
about him. He liked to tell me what I wanted to hear and

his simple way was convincing. I suppose all that was wrong in Willie's world was that nothing matched his dream, the burn was deeper, the crab apple not sweet, the road altogether harder. I might have known that when the farm was reached it would be in temporary occupation. The owners of the place were 'looking' sheep. They had them penned in the steading and were busy treating scab or footrot. Smoke was coming from the chimney. They were heating a meal on the ash-clogged range. Someone was sitting on the corn-chest in the stable.

I had to stifle my eagerness to get my hands on the gun and carry it away. The gun, I may say, was one of those things that belonged to no one. It was part of the unwanted debris left by the previous tenants, but we could hardly commandeer it from under the noses of the new occupants. We sat on the wall and passed the time of day with one of the men working with the penned sheep. He knew we had come for something. To suggest that we might explore the stable wouldn't have been wise. We had to wait. Alas, the work went on in relays, some of the helpers going into the house to get a bowl of soup while others continued with their tasks. Reluctantly we took ourselves off. We had come, we said, in search of a black-faced ram that had climbed out over the march dike. They hadn't seen a black-faced ram because there wasn't one. No help for it, I said to myself, but to come back another day and unearth the fowling piece from the dust and rubble when no one was about.

I was half-way home when I took it into my head to go back alone on the off-chance that the sheep would be done with. I was right. The sheep had gone streaming out from the deserted steading. The shepherds and their helpers were departing. I crouched behind a gorse bush until I thought they were all away and then I slipped out, jumped over the wall into the steading behind the old piggery and made my way round to the stable. The stable was lit by a cobwebbed skylight and a trickle of sunlight through a sliding shutter. I searched behind the corn-chest, and inside it too, but there was nothing! The whole thing was a dream, the sort of story that belonged in the imagination. I went outside and stood looking at the empty courtyard. Someone was in the house. Presently the door opened and one of the sons of the shepherds came out. He wasn't surprised to see me. I explained that I had dropped something and wondered if it lay by the wall where I had been sitting. We talked a little while. I was almost on my way home when the final disappointment came.

'Do you know what they found at the back of the corn-chest?' I was asked.

I knew. An old, eight-bore wildfowling gun, heavy, a bit rusty, but sound. Good enough to stop a greylag twice as far as my own old hammer gun would shoot. I saw the gun a year or two later. It was everything it had been described as being, a goose gun made for a man who loved the estuary, a fowling-piece in the proper sense of the word. It had almost been mine. I have never owned one; I suppose I never shall own one, for that was the gun of my dreams. It had scrolled sideplates and silver-wire inlaying on the fore-end. Its barrel pointed like a high pine tree points to heaven. I could almost have touched the far-up geese with it, it seemed. I never forgot how near I came to owning it by the old rule of finders keepers. Losers weepers, they say. Often after that, if I didn't weep, I sighed.

The modern fowler's gun to which the ancient relics gave place was an altogether more sophisticated weapon. This is the gun the newcomer to the shore will acquire, or covet, according to his fortune. The long and heavy gun may have been put out of fashion by propaganda in favour of magnums and improved cartridges, but the magnum is a heavy gun. Even so the magnum twelve-bore is only a step towards the gun that grandfather needed, the artillery piece to fire perhaps only one or two shots at morning or afternoon flight—and bring down the bird at which it was discharged! The big gun was long in the barrel, large in the bore. It fired ounches of shot. It reached ten or twenty yards farther than ordinary guns and put up a denser hail of lead to strike the far-out goose. This kind of gun you must carry to the morning flight before you are a fowler and know what fowling is. When you carry it the old men of the marsh will keep you company, and also the ghosts who haunt the estuaries they shot half a century or more before you were born, ghosts belonging in the world of Colonel Hawker and his kind.

The four-bore gun is a museum piece. It was made more often for the swivel of a punt than for the shoulder of a man, but there were men who fired four-bores when I was a boy, and thought nothing of it. Most of them rolled on to their backs and had the mud of the marsh under them to withstand the furious blow that a massive fowling-piece weighing perhaps twenty-five pounds inflicted upon the user. Some, it must be said, stood on their feet and fired, blinked and fired again, sometimes. It took a large man to fire such a gun because it was heavy. Few small men can swing and shoot correctly with a gun nearly a quarter of their own weight. If you find such a gun you will see that the breech is like a railway tunnel, the barrel like a rainspout. Fire it if you must. The cartridges are more than difficult to come by. Your friends will tell you that if you don't lie down to use it you may need help, not just to administer first-aid, but to dig your feet out of the mud after the recoil. A lesser piece of ordnance is more in your line.

You may graduate to the long guns of the old fowlers as you discover the elusive ways of geese, first the ten-bore, which is not much more than an outsized twelve, and then the eight-bore, a sturdier and heavier piece of ironmongery. The best of the heavy guns are still those with names like Tolly and Bland. The biggest ten-bore cartridge you can buy will contain little more than an ounce and a half of shot, but the eight-bore cartridge, $4\frac{1}{4}$ inches long, has another ounce of lead in it. When you use this big gun you will fire twice as much lead as you would have in an ordinary twelve-bore gun cartridge. The long gun is heavy. A man who carries one knows he has graduated to the weapon chosen by the professional fowler, a goose gun. It reaches out to the wary bird on the very tail of the bank, to the goose that beats in from the mud and knows exactly how far the ordinary gun can reach. Old fowlers said that it was a gun with knock-down power. There was a special mystique about it that lingers on. A man who owns one of these eight-bore marsh guns and doesn't take it with him knows that he must make a special prayer that the geese will come lower, that they will be wind-harried and slow to gain height.

The man who carries the eight-bore has extra confidence, the magic built into the gun by gunsmiths who specialized in heavy pieces. A day will come when the novice needs this gun, when he believes in nothing less. This is inevitable, just as the coming of the day when he discovers that the long gun is heavy and his body is not made of tough oak and the marsh is getting into his bones. Everything we do ends in compromise, a compromise over mental and physical inability to do what we see others doing. The gun for the goose is one that brings the goose down, a gun in which the fowler believes. The novice believes first what his elders and betters tell him, and then, at last, what his experience has taught him. A man without the long gun may retreat from the marsh and try to shoot the goose as it flies over the hill, or crawl far out into the sands and dig a hole in which he can hide himself so that the geese pass overhead at a more reasonable range. In time he comes to know the size of a goose at

100 feet or 180 feet, and how it looks when it is ten yards beyond range. He will know this, as you will come to know it, when you have watched a hundred flights. The long gun will be slung on your back as for the occasion when the morning is still and the geese climb higher and higher as they talk their way into the morning sun. You may in due time grow out of the longing for such things. I admit that I have taken big guns to the marsh and waited for the occasion when I might justifiably fire at a goose with one of them, but as yet I haven't done so. I dream of the day of the big gun and fowlers whose company I might have been privileged to share. That is enough. To tell the truth, I have shot geese in my imagination with every sort of ancient fowling-piece that was ever used. I have kept company with men who almost died from exposure lying on the frozen shore all night clutching guns made by Joe Manton, but the big gun is not for me, and the only muzzle-loader I possess hangs in my dining-room —to transport me in dreams.

3

Wild Duck

EARLY in your apprenticeship, probably long before you venture out on to the estuary to wait for the flight of the geese, you will learn the ways of the wild duck or, to be explicit and use the name that wasn't used when I was a boy, the mallard. For the mallard is the commonest of our wildfowl, the most sought-after, because it makes a succulent dish and it has this special attraction: to shoot it one need only frequent the common haunts of wildfowl. The mallard uses the river and the riverbank, the ditch, the stream, the quiet pond, the loch, the moorland as well as the far-out muds of the estuary. It lives where it feeds and sometimes it roosts on open water, or perches on the bank and sleeps, or hides itself away in some weeded corner of the brook and flies by night. It breeds in one place and frequents another. One from the next county comes in to a small pool or flashes on your doorstep, while one that was reared on the stream down below may fly to live on some remote estuary in the north.

The magic is there every time two or three duck cross the evening sky and drop their heads as they prepare to land on the pond. With them comes the very fabric of dreams, of places hidden behind the hills, places in the smoky dusk, cold rivers, flooded streams carrying sticks and debris down to the sea, bare willows and stark ash trees; ten, twenty, a hundred miles of country spread in a great carpet of fields, woods and thickets, plough and pasture. Across all of this the flighting mallard may have come. There is a moment or two when the twilight seems to be closing in to complete darkness after the last rays of the sun have died in the western sky. The owl cries and a dog barks. The day is done and at that moment the wild duck comes, swinging round in the bowl of the evening, flying with the urgency of duck approaching a feeding-place. This is something that belongs neither to the day nor to the night, but the timelessness of the hour before absolute darkness and the hour before day has begun to show in the east.

This is when the fowler receives his initiation, contracts something from which he never recovers, nor wants to recover. The experience is brief, but the man who knows it goes home unaware of the hour, of his hunger, the cold-ness of his hands or feet, the tingling of his ears, as though he had lived with his ancestors. Nothing has changed in the night sky, the light dies as it has died since the first light of day. The duck flies as it has always flown, turning, swinging, dropping down, splashing on to the water, swimming to the mud, trundling off to feed; sometimes, when it is disturbed, taking wing again and hurrying up into the night to disappear in a second or two.

This experience is not for everyone. There are people who recognize the duck on an ornamental pond, people who watch its amorous activity along the river on a sunny afternoon, but they may know nothing about the ways of flighting mallard. A fowler who finds himself in the city looks at the duck on the lake in St James's Park and wonders how they flight in and out of the place on winter nights, taking their bearings, perhaps, from illuminated buildings, the tower of Big Ben, the Hilton, or some other landmark, before they wheel to follow the course of the Thames and drop on the tidal mud at Chelsea or water-meadows far beyond Oxford. Perhaps they fly to the Essex marshes, one of the London reservoirs, or a gravel pit out Guildford way? The night belongs to the flying duck. Not many people know what sort of traffic marks the rush hour at twilight and the first combing of the sky at dawn.

The wild duck has its secret life in the open wood where it drops on boggy ground and picks seeds and acorns as well as worms from among the leaves. It feeds in the lying corn of a ruined harvest field, where it gorges grain and works its way deep into the rotting straw, or on the grass field where every night along the flooded places all kinds of things enjoyed by a hungry mallard are to be found in the mud. A mallard belongs to the marsh because the marsh provides food and shelter but it also belongs along the banks of the river below the poultry farm where food that the free-range birds overlook fattens a duck that might otherwise travel far for anything quite so rich. Perhaps in the corner of the pasture the duck discovers sheaves that fell unnoticed from the wagon at harvest time, or it swims out to intercept the titbits some village woman gaily consigns to the brook at the end of her garden.

To be successful in the pursuit of fowl a man must study the species in all its habits. It matters not at all that the duck may only be shot from September until the end of January except below high water mark in the following month, for to know the mallard one must study it wherever it is found, nesting, skulking in the rushes in high summer or flighting to the barley stubbles in the early days of autumn. The mallard nests in spring, of course,

and lays where fancy takes it, in the cover of the heather above the lake, in the low blackberry bush along the stream, in the reeds, or the top of a pollard willow from which the youngsters will tumble and still survive because they are weightless and relaxed.

Look at the mallard's nest with its ten or twelve off-white, faintly blue-tinged eggs and you can hardly fail to realize that the rest of the world about you is as full of wonder and mystery. The eggs are concealed in the soft brownish down the duck has plucked from her breast. Every time the nest is left she covers the eggs and makes her departure with stealth that betrays her concern for the safety of the clutch. When she has gone perhaps ten or twenty yards she walks upright and takes wing. Soon she will be far enough away to deceive anyone about the location of the nest. When she drops down again to return to the eggs she will be devious in her behaviour. If you have searched for the nest of the mallard in the heather you know how near to impossible it is to guess the route the bird is taking. If you have flushed a nesting bird you are hard put to resist the diversion she creates as she lures you from the place, splashing in the water of loch or lake, fluttering and feigning injury as she dives into the reeds. It is an instinct that all sorts of fowl have, but none plays the part better than the mallard until the moment comes to make her own escape and you are left scratching your head and contemplating the fool's task of searching so much undergrowth, such a vast forest of heather or tall reeds, to find the eggs concealed in duck's down.

Study the mallard as she goes to and from her nest and watch how she leads the young away the moment they are water-borne, for she wastes no time in doing this. Almost as soon as the last shell has dried out the brood has vanished. This is because a waterbird has many enemies. A fox will search the marsh for the duck's nest. The carrion crow patrolling overhead may miss the eggs hidden in

their covering of down, but the crow and the black-backed
gull, to say nothing of the stoat, the rat, the heron and
other ravenous creatures, will search for the dappled duck-
lings from the moment they hatch until they can fend for
themselves on open water. The mallard has been conditioned to persecution since the first swamp island showed
above water and it has survived because it has discovered
how to survive. It is wary, watchful, keen-sighted, a
master of the art of taking cover and getting away without
making a disturbance. This is the fowl you must study if
you are to be a fowler, the elusive bird of the reeds and
rushes, the bird of the night and half light, the bird that
sometimes walks abroad on the inundated pasture and
takes wing from the ditch when you least expect it. When
it comes from the barley stubble it is better to eat than any
sort of bird a man may shoot for his dinner. This was discovered when man had nothing better to shoot with than
a bow and arrow.

Duck were feeding and flying by night long before
you and I thought about going to the marsh with a gun
or our great-grandfathers primed their fowling-pieces.
The fowlers who haunted the marshes to ply their trade
and supply the market with duck in the days when
fowling-pieces were primitive and crude had other ways
of taking them. They lay in the creeks and drains and
studied the duck as they swam to and fro feeding in the
fringes of the reeds and sifting the mud for delicacies they
loved best. They saw the way duck travelled upstream and
down, how they crossed obstacles or swam under them,
and they set snares for them, snares and traps of different
sorts. Here the old fowler would bait the stream with little
potatoes or scatter barley to make the duck come in and
when they were accustomed to the place he would set lines
with hooks and bait in the same way as he fished for carp
or bream. The wild duck would take the hook and sit on
the water moored until the fowler came to collect them.

Sometimes the shallows would be dotted with gin traps to take the mallard as they dipped to lift the bait from the gravel. The cunning catcher of fowl would string nets to hang vertically across the creek, one a heavy cord net of a large size and the other two making a sort of sandwich of it, hanging on either side, smaller and finer-meshed nets. When the duck came hurrying up the stream, disturbed from the lower reaches, they would be bagged in the heavy net, pocketed by the mesh of the finer net, each one ready to be lifted out and despatched. If duck flighted up or down it made little difference. The heavy net was well braced, the smaller-meshed nets were large enough in area to make a score of pouches if twenty duck were caught. Once in the net the duck couldn't move and the catching went on so long as fowl travelled the course of the stream. Mallard, however, frequently swim along a stream and prefer to travel in this way unless put to flight. The most cunning fowler had his way of snaring them, even though they might swim with their necks outstretched and barely above the water, for they could be made to swim as he wanted them to swim by tying a fairly stout cord across the water close to the surface. Encountering the barrier swimming birds would duck underneath and pop up on the other side. This ensured that they held their heads at the right height for the brief moment or two in which they encountered nooses dangling from a second and slightly higher cord. Some birds, of course, would miss the noose and swim on, but a few yards farther upstream there would be another barrier and a second string of dangling horsehair snares and perhaps a little farther on still a third and then a fourth. The wild duck may well have been hunted into the cover of the night by the savage with the spear and the bow and arrow, but it was no safer in the darkness!

There was another way that the bird-catcher adopted when he was hard put to it to earn his living. He would lay a network of heavily limed cord to entangle the duck as they dropped into a pool or a creek. The lime was made from the boiled bark of the holly bush, a nauseous green mess that entangled the feet and feathers of birds coming in contact with the cord. It didn't matter that the handsome mallard drake lost its painted beauty. Soon after it was caught it was plucked and dressed for the dealer's slab. The marsh fed the town. The fowler was responsible for bringing duck to the table. It didn't matter how it was done and the old methods had the merit of being silent although they were much more brutal than the blunderbuss.

Such ways are long since discontinued. The professional fowler, like the professional poacher, has vanished from the scene, or plies his trade in the face of difficulties that make earning a living harder and harder with every season that passes. It may not add much to your useful education in fowling to learn that these things were done, or how they were done, but they are part of the lore of the business like the old guns.

There is only one way to get a wild duck for your dinner today and that is with the gun. No man worthy of the name of fowler would buy a duck from a dealer or, indeed, sell his bag or shoot more than he and one or two friends might be able to eat. It cannot be denied that there are people who shoot duck for something more than the satisfaction of eating what they shoot. But it is not to make you a marksman, a mere killer of fowl, that I would persuade you to follow my steps in the world of fowling; far from it. There is no excuse for indiscriminate slaughter and perhaps no great excuse for a man who earns his living in any of the every-day trades or professions going out to get his dinner, for killing is done for us behind closed doors. Meat is made remote from blood and death as a potato in polythene is remote from the good earth. There is no excuse—except that man hunts one thing or hunts another. At least it is more wholesome to hunt one's dinner than hunt a rival out of his contentment.

I went to flight duck when I had my first gun. I was a country boy and I was aware that life lives on life and there is a law governing things like the birth of a calf that will go to be slaughtered, and the way one creature preys upon another. The duck, I discovered, were coming to the corn. We had been harvesting on the hill for several days before the weather broke and everything had to be abandoned for the time being, the horses put out to grass, the binder sheets covered in sheaves, the knives brought home for sharpening and the scythe hung in the shed. Everything that had to be brought home had been brought home, it seemed, until Wee Johnnie remembered that his tattered waistcoat had been left on the drystone wall. In the pocket of his waistcoat was his watch. It was safe enough, for no one would touch the old waistcoat or take the watch, but Wee Johnnie feared that the rain would do the works of his watch no good. He persuaded me to walk all the way up to the far corner of the field and bring back his waistcoat. He was milking and I had nothing better to do. I walked up through the wet field along the path the binder had cut. The waistcoat was where it had been thrown, but before I reached it I was startled by the wild duck that swept over the wall, almost dropped into the standing corn, hung in the air for a moment, and then climbed away again. There were at least ten in the flight. I carried on to the place where the waistcoat draped the stones and a second flight skimmed over my head and settled in the corn. Five more came as I stood in the dusk wondering what I should do about them. It was too dark and much too late for me to go down to the house and come back with the gun, but if nothing changed, if it rained to-morrow and the duck were still as hungry for corn, I could come up and shelter behind the wall and perhaps shoot one as it came to feed.

The thought of shooting a duck gripped me. I could hardly sleep for thinking about it. The next day I watched the rain clouds moving slowly across the hill, big, brown-bellied clouds that were in no hurry to reach the far side of the bay. I looked at the gun more than once, checked the cartridges, used the pull-through and waited impatiently for evening. I was up on the cornfield long before the light had begun to fade, long before they were half-way through the milking. I watched the distant meadows, the outline of the river. Every bird that flew from one field to another had my keenest attention and I hardly knew how to contain myself as the evening drew on, the watery sunset died and the haze of rain spread across familiar fields and farmsteads. I held the gun and didn't feel the chill of the barrels, the rain on my hands. The hollow sound of pigeons cooing in the low planting died away at last and twilight came. The duck must have missed their landmarks, it seemed, for they were a long time arriving. When they did come they gave no warning. All at once, before I saw them properly or could put up the gun, they were down in the corn, invisible. I almost choked with excitement. Should I jump to my feet and try to shoot one as they took flight? I debated with myself until the excitement became almost unbearable, but then it happened, a solitary drake came in directly over my head, swept across the field and came back towards me, slowing down, looking for the rest of the duck that had arrived before him. He posed for a moment, wings spread, body almost vertical, neck outstretched. I put up the gun and fired. He dropped into the corn. A dozen others flew up and away, some of them making a rasping quack as they took fright and rushed off. I wasn't able to fire a second shot. It was a minute or two before I recovered and plunged into the corn to find the drake. He was there, all right, tucked down in the flattened stalks of oats, but not hard to see, even in the half light. I pounced on him. I had shot a duck for my dinner, a corn-fat wild duck I had discovered in its feeding-place. I had flighted wild duck for the first time. I knew something about the fowler's excitement, the hackle-raising, heart-pounding reaction of the hunter.

4

Walking Water-meadows

THE water-meadow, in case you are unfamiliar with it, is one of the older devices of those who have cultivated riverside land since man first began to farm. There are, however, thousands of acres of water-meadow that bear no more important crop these days than hay and supplementary grazing for cattle; beds of sedge encroach upon the meadows, and bushes and stunted trees take over, slowing the draining of the fields, creating a place in which the river floods and eddies until it carpets the higher ground with dead grass, rushes, straw, twigs and branches. Some of the older water-meadows have lost their title for they have become bog in which mace and tall reeds grow. Red-stemmed marsh plants spread their seeds, rattling like pepper pots, showering anyone who passes with a hail of hard seed which falls into the water and never grows but lies there to feed whatever creatures live in the jungle, duck and waterhen, coot, vole and mice. The very nature of such places makes them forbidding when the river rises and gently eases hay ricks from their resting-places or backs a barrier óf flotsam into the mouth of the drain, stopping the flow, making the ditches far back in the more arable land overflow at the cattle drinking-holes. The duck of the river haunt the water-meadows. There is no better place to find them than in the secret corners of the alders away down where the drains have to be crossed warily on treacherously slippery planks or poles covered with a scraping of earth to provide a foothold.

Duck that frequent the water-meadows travel up and down the river at different times of day. They live in the cress-beds, the steep-sided ditches where the long grass waves in the current and reflects the mood of the river down below when days of rain have produced a flood. The duck here are undisturbed except perhaps when a fox explores the alders and paddles his way along the river's course, or an otter swims out of the current and heads up the ditch to corner some misguided fish in search of a spawning-ground. The duck has its enemies, and even in the deeper water of the drain an old pike may lie moored to intercept the young brood trailing across the surface behind the mother bird.

The man who would shoot a duck is half-way to success when he has access to such places. He can walk the meadows in thigh boots and waylay the duck on their daily flights up and down the main watercourse, flush fowl from the reeds and alders and discover the feeding-places of mallard that come in early and stay late in the morning. One shot may put a hundred duck in the air at once and away they will go, seeming to have deserted the meadows once and for all as they sweep out over the willows, swing round to follow the water and seem to diminish in size, or disappear beyond some natural barrier in the valley. The morning sun shines bravely through rain-clouds and glints on the water. A coot croaks in the reeds and a sizable log goes rolling and tumbling down the river and there never was a time that seemed more unlikely for the success of the fowler waiting in the meadow, but in an hour or so the sound of the gun will have been forgotten. Snipe will move in the rushes and a rat swim across the drain and the duck come back again, beating their way high overhead, perhaps, or keeping to the far bank, prospecting over the meadows nevertheless, and searching for others they lost during the alarm.

Stand very still and look at the waterlilies. Watch the circling flight only from the very corner of your eye and keep your face averted from them. They look once perhaps, but the keen sight of a duck will detect the slightest movement, the slightest contrast in the background of reeds and rushes and the pasture beyond. The time to move is when the flight is almost upon you; move smoothly, with determination, and remember that you must swing with the flight and overtake the bird you aim to bring down before you pull the trigger. Remember, too, that the river is deep and treacherous. If the duck falls in the current it may sail away to the bend on the far side and come across again to rest in the outermost edge of the alders where no one dares venture to recover it. Mark the falling bird well and let the flight go on. It isn't always easy to find a duck in the water-meadow. Even when the dead bird is located the shortest way to it may involve a devious route up the side of a deep ditch with crumbling banks, across an apron of rusty barbed wire and back again to the riverbank. There are aids to the recovery of duck that have been shot, water-spaniels and retrievers of different breeds, and ingenious appliances that can be thrown or catapulted so that the dead bird can be raked in or dragged across the water to the man who would put it in his bag.

There was a time when, trusting to neither dog nor

line, I would plunge into the water and flounder and struggle through to pick up my kill, but often I found the exercise dangerous, my legs encountering mud like porridge, my feet becoming held fast in hidden, greasy clay, or stumbling on the submerged branches of trees. The man who sees his duck floating away may resolve not to shoot when he has little chance of recovering what he has killed. This is a sound resolution for anyone, whether he shoots on the marsh, on the estuary or in the water-meadows. Once I took an eager fowler to the water-meadows I had often visited in my youth and had to forcibly restrain him from jumping into the river to bring back a mallard drake I had carelessly shot when it was over the water. There was some small excuse, perhaps, for we had had a frustrating week on the mudbanks waiting for geese that always came off too high. My companion badly wanted something to take home with him. We fared no better on the water-meadows. The place had been shot too often and the duck that remained were wild and quick to go. Down at the junction of the widest and deepest drain and the river proper, I stepped forward into a forest of tall reeds and the drake took wing almost from beneath my feet. He was a good way out over the river when I fired but he was quite dead, for he floated heavily and turned slowly round and round as the current carried him away. My companion looked at me and asked me if I intended to let the river claim my bird. I nodded but a moment later I had to grab him by the arm as he threw down his gun and prepared to jump into the water. What sort of a fowler was I when I wouldn't risk the river? I was asked. I shook my head. I knew my river. It looked anything but treacherous, flowing unhurriedly past the weeds at the bend, carrying a feather on the surface of its peaty water. I knew its pace at the bend, its undertow and the way it hurried a struggling sheep away down to the sea, past the stone bridge, under the overhanging elms and oaks and on, faster and faster, to the hills of sand and the white line of the turning tide.

We walked the meadows to overtake the duck but it was useless for the dead bird was hung up in the fork of a tree growing far out from the bank. My companion ventured a little too far and his thigh boots filled. He poured them out and shivered. It was colder than he had thought, much colder. The mallard drake might rise from the branch when rain brought another flood but there was no way of dislodging it. Late in the afternoon we intercepted a flight of greylags crossing the meadows. When we fired at them they obliged by coming round a second time but I made sure they were inside the meadows and not over the river before I put up the gun. My companion may have allowed himself to be persuaded that it wasn't worth his while risking his life for a duck but I wasn't sure that I could hold him back from the river if a goose happened to drop on the water.

Water-meadows have a special allure for me because I was tantalized by them when I was a boy. Every year the flooded meadows could be seen from the higher fields of the farm. I am not sure now whether the meadows were still being flooded deliberately to fertilize the land as was the custom or whether they simply flooded automatically with the rising of the river in the wet months of the year, but without fail I would see the glint of water on those flat green meadows and long to be allowed to go down there. All sorts of stories were told to frighten me away. Not only boys, but men, had been taken by the flooded river. Carts of hay, haystacks and wooden out-buildings were moved from the meadows overnight. The river took them by stealth and the big drains had drowned many a horse of seventeen or eighteen hands. No one with any sense would go down there when the river could rise, fill the ditches and drains and cut off a man's escape route in a short time, but I hardly listened to these grim warnings. I

watched the distant waterholes. I could see the duck resting on them, hundreds of duck at times. I could see them
going out across the meadows on the far side, circling the
farm isolated on a mound marked by two or three pine
trees. The people who lived there, it seemed to me, lived
in paradise. Duck sailed round them and splashed into the
water almost on their doorstep. Anyone living there could
shoot a duck whenever he had the mind to, and were they
not neighbours who might be persuaded to grant me the
privilege of shooting one or two? I pleaded to be allowed
to go but it was a long time before my pleas were
effective. The river was more than a wide, winding watercourse coming through little green hills topped by fir
plantings and going on down among bracken slopes and
thick woods of ash and oak and elm, past the distillery,
under the bridge by the creamery, and out below the railway line, to the bay. It was a kind of a monster. It looked
like a snake and it coiled itself about things that came
within its reach. An old friend of my grandfather's had
been drowned one night coming home from the town. The
river was evil, cold and baleful like the gedds, the big
green pike that lived down there beyond the lily-pads and
between the water-meadows.

A time comes for everyone who waits. In due course I
found my own way to the water-meadows, first to fish in
the river and the burn that joined it, and then to shoot. I
was never more fascinated. The duck sprang into the air
at every turn, calling in alarm as they went. Teal there
were by the dozen at times, especially when the weather
had been cold, for teal are fond of shelter and the banks of
the river had been built high above the meadows to limit
the flooding. In cold weather the meadows were alive with
fowl, even though it was often almost impossible to move
up to them without getting drenched to the skin and claw-
ing one's way out of ditches, the banks of which had
crumbled and fallen in. I couldn't resist going down when-

ever the opportunity presented itself and for a long time
I believed that these meadows were unique. Later I came
to know others, meadows with more cultivation, less peaty
water, broad beds of cress and safer and sounder paths
and little bridges, but the water-meadows of my boyhood
have never lost their magic even though I may no longer
visit them.

I went down in the company of Jimmie who was drawn
to the river as I was, promising to carry whatever was shot
and not fall into a hole that would take me over the ears,
for then what report could be given but that I was
drowned and the river had taken me the way it took sheep
and cows and coops of chickens when it was in the mood?
It seems to me now that there were more duck on every
meadow that day than I ever saw again. Perhaps this was
so. It may have been that the cold wet weather had
brought a migrant population to compete with the duck
that normally lived there. We stepped across the first
slippery plank and walked down the bank beyond it and
three drakes flew into the air. I gasped, for the drakes
crossed the meadow, drawing others up to join them until
the noise of duck bursting up from the rushes, the grass
and the reeds seemed to fill my head with sound. I looked
here and there, startled again and again as the blurred outlines of escaping fowl caught my eye. I saw duck plastered
against the clouds overhead, silhouetted against the morning sun, flying at all angles. The noise of Jimmie's shot
almost stopped my heart. I saw nothing fall but how he
missed hitting a duck I cannot tell. It was several minutes
before the meadow and the field beyond were not being
crossed by duck and away they went, high into the morning. Jimmie stood and stared.

'My!' he said. 'I'll never see the like of that again!'

I had never seen its like before. I had never in all my
dreams of the place seen so many duck.

A little while later a single drake which had been sulk-

ing in the reeds took off. Jimmie shot it, but it was only
winged and went splashing across the meadow, a sad and
sorry sight. Jimmie took to his heels after it and called on
me to make haste for it might take some catching. A duck
that is wounded can still run, you will discover. It can run
almost as fast as a hare at times. Jimmie came to the first
big ditch and almost had the bird, but it flapped across
the water and quickly scuttled up the far bank. I looked
at the obstacle and the way the water was flowing to the
river with such urgency and decided that I couldn't risk
falling in if my jump didn't quite take me to the far bank.
Jimmie, whose legs were longer, hurled himself across but
slipped back and in. The ditch was deeper than either of
us had thought because Jimmie's jacket, which he had left
unbuttoned, floated out on a level with his shoulders. The
gun slipped from his hand. He gulped and gasped and
clawed himself to safety. The gun wasn't out of reach
because it had lodged on some obstruction below the surface and he hauled it out as he crawled to safety. The duck
had run on. Jimmie had no heart to follow it but I had
discovered a way over. There was a slippery plank bridge
a little lower down. Across the plank I went as fast as I
could go.

A mallard drake in winter plumage is a rich sort of
peaty brown on the back. Its head is green but nothing
can disguise the white brand on the wings or the white
signal of its tail and rump. I saw the drake crossing the
inundated meadow and knew that I had to reach it before
it made the thicket of willow, the green sallow that grew
all along the far ditch. It was a close thing. I threw myself
down and caught the duck just before it reached the cover.
It flapped and beat my face with its wings. Jimmie came
squelching over to make an end of it.

The duck that we had put up not long before were
coming back in waves, some high up and far out but
others low and seeking places in which to drop. Jimmie

cocked the gun and fired but again he was unsuccessful. I watched him rubbing his ear and wondered what was wrong.

'Did you see what happened?' he asked.

I shook my head. It seemed that mud or some other sort of obstruction had got down the barrel of the gun. When Jimmie fired the ring of the suppressed explosion had all but deafened him. It was something less terrifying than a barrel bursting, of course, for that might have put paid to Jimmie for good, but it made me shiver. A duck wasn't worth being drowned for and a man with his head blown off never walked a water-meadow again!

We agreed to say nothing about the incident. Jimmie carried the duck and I carried the gun. He was finding things a little difficult. It was hard enough to wade through waterlogged fields, but when one's clothes were heavy and saturated with peaty water it told on a man's strength. The flying duck had gone again. I took the cartridge from the gun and made sure there was no obstruction before I reloaded. Jimmie rubbed his ear and shivered. He was anxious to get home and change his clothes but I wanted to stay and have my turn. We stood in the shelter of a hawthorn tree growing on the high bank of the river, a position from which we could see a long way in both directions. The duck were a long time coming back. Half of them had found new shelter somewhere else, it seemed, but those that came were satisfied that danger had passed. I waited until they were across the bank and clear of the drain. It wasn't as difficult to shoot them flying in as I had thought it might be. They passed at an angle, dropping. I swung the gun and picked my bird. It dropped and the remainder climbed, splitting up into twos and threes, radiating from the meadow as they had done before. We had a duck and a drake. But Jimmie's teeth were chattering. We lost no time in getting across the meadow, over the fence near the elm trees and on up

across the harder ground, through the store cattle to the
gate and the road. An old man was pushing a bicycle up a
slope. He stopped to watch us as we emerged on to the
public highway.

'Down getting yourselves a couple of jukes, boys?' he
inquired.

Jimmie grunted a reply and I smiled. After all, I was
dry. The water wasn't pouring from my wet trousers and
squelching in my boots as I walked. That was the first
time and a day would come when I would stand waistdeep
in the water waiting for ducks in the same place with a
cold east wind bringing tears to my eyes.

5

Birds in the Barley

A FIELD of barley is a richer sight to look upon than a field of oats, though it lacks the beauty of wheat because there is something full and wholesome about the golden wheat dotted with those red poppies that somehow always manage to get sown in a wheatfield. The barley is combed by the wind. It has less resistance to the wind than the stronger wheat. It goes down much easier and becomes what is known as straw-broken. Farmers will tell you that strong barley is nearly always short in the straw. The man who cultivates barley with a good head and long, strong straw will make his fortune. Barley lies in places where oats still manage to rise. Almost everyone who grows the crop looks anxiously at his field when there had been a late summer gale. The havoc of the wind needs to be seen to be believed. The slope of a barley field can look like the tousled head of a boy newly risen from bed—except that it can never be straightened again. The knives of the binder will crop the heads and they will tumble to the ground, the combine will drag the straw by its roots and men will have to take time to clear the great harvesting machine of clods of grass and soil and tangled straw. A good malting barley is a precious crop. Distillers and brewers buy the grain before it has sprouted but he is a lucky man who cuts a whole field without losing a bushel or two, even in a summer when the sun shines and the corn is cut with little loss of time. The barley field attracts more than the contractor and the combine team. It lures the birds. Partridges and pheasants walk through the fallen corn and fill their crops, and at nightfall—the duck come.

Let me urge you, if you are an apprentice to the business of fowling, to walk the summer lanes and learn to know a barley field when you see one. Having discovered the field, approach the farmer and ask him about the duck that come to his field at evening. There is hardly a barley field that isn't visited by mallard in the late summer. You may be turned away, for a man who has broken straw doesn't want more of his crop trodden down and destroyed by someone lumbering across his field to search for a duck he has shot. Convince the farmer that you are a responsible fellow. Tell him that you have a keen and light-footed dog which you will keep in check and release only when a duck has been brought down. He may listen to you, for flights of mallard dropping into the barley all night long may take as much grain as the first few yards of the field the combine cuts the following morning.

Duck and barley go together as duck goes with green peas or orange sauce. There is no tastier bird a man can eat than a young summer duck shot on the barley field. Strangely enough, the barley field's secret remains a secret as far as some unobservant fowlers are concerned. You must live in a place where barley is grown to discover for yourself the dusk activity of flighting mallard, a September miracle, the magic of an autumn evening when the night-jar is still flying and the cottage lights are coming on while their roofs are still touched by the sinking sun.

Barley for the distillery occupied a fair acreage on some of the farms round about when I was a boy. I don't remember being told that wild duck love barley above anything else and that if oats and barley grow in adjoining fields it is in the barley that the hungry duck will be cropping grain.

Wait for the duck and give yourself good time. In the early days of autumn they come early, perhaps an hour before dusk, sometimes earlier. After the young duck have grown big enough to fend for themselves they gather on the wider pools of the river, the loch or lake, where they can roost by day. At evening a restlessness gets into them and they begin to move, splashing about after each other, taking short flights and dropping down again until one of the older birds rises, and away they go, out over the countryside to their feeding-ground. It is a strange thing that some birds fly in one direction and others in another almost as though they had an instinctive knowledge of the locality in which barley is being grown. There must be a first time, each year, when mallard begin to flight to the cornfield and perhaps the prospecting is done by older birds that fly by day. I am inclined to think that, even though the pattern of cultivation changes, some duck have a recollection of fields in which, in other years, they found their favourite crop. A barley stubble to which duck flight in one season is a field to which duck will come if only once or twice in the next summer because there is corn growing, though the farmer may have changed his plan and seeded a field with oats. Even if the field is turned back to pasture duck will come to it at odd times, just as they show a liking for pastures on which no crop other than grass was ever grown, though they don't visit every field and a haunt of duck remains distinctively a haunt of duck.

The ways of some farmers are almost as hard to explain as the ways of fowl for I have known them to go on seeding a field with barley when in the previous year they were only able to harvest a small proportion of the crop, hardly enough to call a yield at all, and not much more than the seed sown. No fowler would question such a man about his reason for persisting in planting barley. Duck come because barley is something they can hardly resist and men plant barley perhaps because they remember the years of plenty rather than the years of famine. Next year, they say hopefully, perhaps the wind won't knock it all down and the price of good malting barley will be better. There never was summer without wind and rain, but rain swells the grain and flattens the straw—and beats it down. The wind that dries the barley breaks its stalks.

The fowler feels that he is doing something useful by waiting for the duck, and he is being useful, for no farm-yard duck ever ate more greedily than a mallard down among the lying corn. I have watched them in the twilight, hurrying after each other as they tumble into the corn. They swarm to the feast, ducks and drakes, all as hungry as can be, all determined to gorge until they can hardly rise. Stand and clap your hands, as I have done, and the grey sky is criss-crossed with fleeing mallard, mallard complaining as they go hurrying aloft to fly in a great circle and come back in again, flying low and taking advantage of their background, skimming the hedges, gliding, rolling down and dropping, sometimes with hardly a sound.

Take the old dog with you or you will hardly find a single duck you shoot. This is the penalty of shooting in the gathering gloom of nightfall and if you take no dog you will have to rely on your ability to judge where the duck fell in a sea of broken straw. What is more, the duck, if they happen not to have been cleanly killed, will wriggle under cover and lie there undetected, though you pass them and walk over them a dozen times. Unless he is a very obedient dog, make sure that you have a leash with you to restrain him. He will feel your excitement when duck come in on the other side of the field, or out of range, and want to rush out to flush them. Keep him under control and control your own shaking limbs. Remember that the first duck in, if they are beyond the range of your gun, act as decoys for the next arrivals. Sit tight and move as little as possible. If you are on the stubble for the first time you may construct a hide for yourself from the lying sheaves or build one from the straw bales dropped by the combine. You will make sure that you are hidden from approach from all sides and that some semblance of cover screens your upturned face. Duck miss very little when they are coming round in the reconnaissance circuit that precedes their dropping. Sometimes a single bird will come over wide and far out and go away again. I have often thought that this bird led the subsequent flight, but occasionally, when birds have not been disturbed on the stubbles before, they will fly in directly and drop without making any precautionary circuit.

It may be that you will find it too difficult to arrange straw bales or gather sheaves in the most likely area, in which case you must take to the hedgerow or the shelter of a tree and build a rough sort of hide for yourself with whatever materials are at hand. I have camouflaged myself with dock and ragwort, trimmed myself and decorated my head and shoulders with thorn, foxglove, long grass and strands of honeysuckle or bindweed. I have knitted hides from branches and sprays of green foliage fastened together with string or soft iron wire and convinced myself that I looked like a bush or a clump of weeds and small birds have perched upon me but I have afterwards been dismayed to find that the duck for some reason didn't like the bush or the weedpatch and settled two or three hundred yards farther down the field. This is something that has a simple answer. Flighting mallard are suspicious of everything and anything new and unfamiliar. Bales of straw and the silent combine sitting on the stubble hold no terror for the flighting duck inspecting the field from three or four hundred feet up in the evening sky but a bush in the middle of a stubble is a conspicuous object. A hide should be an extension of some larger bush or tree, area of weeds, or stone-heap.

The early days of September will bring duck to the cornfield well before sunset, but as the evenings draw in and the young duck of the season become more familiar with the hazards which may be encountered on the stubbles they will flight later and come in more and more in the dusk. There is a drawback to twilight shooting that many a novice finds baffling. A duck in the gathering darkness sometimes looks within range when it is not. It seems to fly at a reasonable height and yet it flies on unharmed when the report of the gun has died. Perspective in the half-light is hard to judge. A mallard looks as big as a goose when it crosses the grey patch between the ash trees, and as small as a teal when one follows another quickly down into the corn. Furthermore all duck look black at night. On a misty autumn evening they sometimes look much larger than they really are. On chilly, starlit evenings they look small. On bright moonlight nights they are often hardest of all to measure. Only time, days spent out in the open acquiring instinctive judgement, can remedy the fact that often leads to a fowler talking about selling his gun or buying more powerful cartridges.

The advantage of the twilight surely lies in the fact that the man on the stubbles needs to give little thought to camouflaging himself, so long as he takes care not to silhouette himself on the skyline or stand like a statue on the fence. A thorn tree, tall broom or gorse will conceal your presence, so long as your hands and face aren't too white. No one would wait for duck in conspicuous clothes —white hat, a light-coloured coat, a cricket pullover— but many a man who wears drab green forgets that his hands betray him as he begins to lift the gun and his face is a signal to the incoming duck when he stares up and screws his eyes to separate the birds' blurred outlines from the dark cloud that hangs behind them. There is nothing more dismaying than to see the duck turn away from the stubble and know that some slight movement betrayed your presence. When this happens there is a lesson to be learned, a lesson in self-control and fieldcraft. To be sure of one's self one must learn to be as steady at the flight as the most carefully trained dog, to circle the field with the duck, seeing what they see, the black border of the hedge, the ash tree, the patch of broom on the grass bank at the bottom of the field, the gate and the gorse growing along the high bank above the drystone wall. Duck search the area in front of them and movement betrays a man more readily than anything else.

There is virtually nothing more exciting than a vigil on the stubble for the first time in a season. No matter what information one may have or what recollections of flights in another season persist in the mind, things are never the same as they were yesterday or last year. Who can predict what mallard will do when they flight in different ways in varying conditions of weather? Consider how hard it is for them to find their landmarks and flight line in fog, and how protracted the flight can be when the whole countryside is bathed in moonlight which enables them to fly where they like when they like! On a rainy evening they may come early. On a bright sunny evening with a lingering red sunset they may be high and late and, in spite of all the layers of experience of a score of seasons, this time the nagging doubt suggests they may not come at all!

Fowlers who love to flight duck do so hopefully. Many of them acquire an instinct which tells them that duck will come on a particular evening, sooner or later. If this judgement proves ill-founded on a certain occasion the circumstances are studied and every incident and feature of the occasion weighed. Didn't it begin to rain and the wind died when the rain began? Could that have had something to do with it? Was it warmer or colder, more like thunder? Time passes with this kind of speculation.

The mystery remains, and no man can ever have the complete answer, but wait for that first flight and listen to the sounds that mark the closing of the day, the milking machines purring away in shippons of farms round about, children laughing as they ride a ramshackle bicycle on the road, the blare of a motor horn, the lowing of a cow and the cry of curlew going away down to the seaboard meadows. The partridges converse in a rasping call that marks the hour when they roost in the long grass out in the middle of the field, a pheasant complains when something puts him to flight, and in the meantime the sky darkens a shade. The fields belong to the browsing sheep. The last tractor has rumbled to a standstill, the last poultry-house has been closed. The bat is under the hedgeside trees, darting through the milling insects. The swallows and swifts have gone, and a barn owl sits on the fencepost unsure whether it is time to patrol the edge of the stubble for mice or beat across the forestry tract to find a vole.

The duck are coming, an echelon of them, black shapes in formation climbing out across the intervening marshland, an invasion of bombers coming at dusk, but they hold course and pass on away over to the left. As they go another flight, farther out, is spotted on its way to some other familiar stubbling ground. The flight that comes in at last nearly passes the field and then swings over the ash trees, almost touching the mountain of old hay along the hedge and spreading out, six or eight feet from the top of the uncut barley. Will more come or should someone stand up and clap his hands? The duck that are down stay down. In a minute, like that frantic time on the lake when trout begin to feed all at once, a dozen mallard are overhead, behind them a second and a third formation, planing in, wings outstretched, lulled into unwariness by all the mallard already on the corn. The time has come. Stand up and shoot! Mark the bird as it loses height and just clears the hedge to thud on to the grass field beyond. Turn and try to make it a brace, and then settle back into the grass and relax for a little while. The duck are a mile away, far out over the open countryside, flying fast but turning to come back, for this is something they haven't encountered before. They will return to the barley once, twice, perhaps three times, fewer each time perhaps, but some will come in, and they will be the plump succulent mallard of the stubbles, fit for the table of a gourmet!

It is momentary, this experience. No one lives at the same pitch of excitement for a long period of time. When it is over the untimed seconds are fixed in the mind, implanted indelibly so that you will remember them without effort in five or ten years. This is the great fascination of fowling, the transfixed images, a duck flying at an unbelievable speed across a sky streaked grey and pale yellow and tinted red at the horizon, and another one tumbling to the stubbles, the flash at the muzzle of the gun when night is almost down, the sound of the dog's progress through the long grass as he comes back with the duck in his jaws, the small seeds from the dock rolling between neck and shirt-collar, the smell of powder and the faint, far-away sound of some iron-shod implement being trundled along a hard road. If you understand none of this I have persuaded you to travel in a world in which you don't really belong, but if you do you have the blood of our ancestors in your veins and the instincts of the hunter. I would not change the evenings I have spent sitting in the hedge alongside a barley stubble for all the sophisticated entertainment the world has to offer.

6

The Lure of the Marsh

WHETHER you shoot the stubbles or not, and stubble shooting is of necessity a limited thing, you will graduate to the marsh, for the variety of the marsh in situation and topographical detail has within it everything that the heart could desire. The place for partridge is the pasture or the rootfield, for the eagle the crag, for the duck the marsh, and the beauty of marshland is its unspoilt state, its unchanged appearance through generations and perhaps centuries of time. As the fisherman pauses to look at every river, stream or lake his eye encounters, the dedicated fowler halts to weigh up the haunts of duck and the fascination of things he cannot see holds him while he conjures up his dreams. Here, perhaps, he stands in poor farming country, in a valley into which streams drain without finding a river to carry away their spate, and the land is ill drained, the cart tracks and mud-rutted roads are full of potholes, the verges deep and soft, so that anyone who walks on the grass feels the water rising at the pressure of his foot. The hedges are unkempt, the willows flourish along with bog myrtle and warty birch, alders, blackthorns and hazels that shelter the flashes, waterholes and brooding pools so that they ice up only in the extreme cold of winter.

In such places duck breed along with other water fowl, for they are the poet's 'haunt of coot and hern', the marsh harrier, the falcon, the hawk. In the reeds the bittern calls and one day he is seen, a down-looker with his beak pointing at the sky so that he can watch the watcher in front of him. The marsh may be large, an endless wilderness of grass and rampant scrub and briar along a depression that might have been a riverbed, but silted up with peat and sand and soil from the hillsides, a jungle for the brown hare and the fox, the water rail, the lynx-like cat gone wild, migrant birds of all kinds, or it may be a small and private world of a few acres closed in by deep drains, a place where no cattle may venture and no one cares to lay tiles or even dig ditches to carry off the surface water. In the black earth of the marsh snipe are never without feeding-places, duck can feed and paddle and the surrounding scrub trees give cover.

There must be hundreds of marshes frequented at night by duck without anyone ever dreaming that fowl visit them, places that lie undiscovered, like ponds in which big tench swim or carp break the surface only after dark on warm summer evenings. The fowler's explorations are encouraged once in a while when he flushes a duck from a pool in the middle of one of these jungles and sees the marks of many more, droppings on the mud, feathers blown to the side of the pool by a gentle breeze, footprints on the bank, nest-like resting-places in the long grass.

Once in a while, the novice, inquiring for a place to flight mallard, will be told that someone working on one of the fields has often seen duck sailing over in the twilight, heading for the boggy corner beyond the drain. The information may be reliable but when it is checked the duck have as often as not for some reason forsaken the place for a day or two. No one can expect reward without effort. Another twilight flight on the marsh may hold the answer, although another two or three flights may hardly be enough, but a place for duck has all the marks to show, weed and water, mud, shelter, a flighting space—that is, open access in at least one direction, for duck will hardly ever frequent a place they have difficulty in leaving when disturbed. Go down to the marsh and make yourself comfortable on an old stump, having made sure that you know exactly where you walked when you came on to the ground. Landmarks are important if you are to remain dry and escape the danger of going into bog or quicksand, or drowning in a waterhole. Mark the tall trees in relation to the way out, and the small things beside the path, so that if need be you can identify them like milestones when you are stumbling on the road back. Take heed of everything significant in relation to the direction in which you are facing and wait without moving about.

The duck, if they are coming, will arrive when you least expect them. They may pass overhead and come back in after turning round a landmark. Duck have this habit. You may find it difficult to get within range of them because they drop down in a place far out in waterlogged ground, but if you watch how they approach that particular flash or flooded place you will discover that invariably they find it by first sighting another topographical feature, the tops of tall trees round which they always turn, or perhaps a single tree that gives them a line on the place where they will eventually drop. Only experience will offer you these secrets.

Many a man who has flighted for years doesn't really understand this orientation business. Duck will change the direction of their approach and fly differently in different conditions of weather, but like homing pigeons or migrating birds of almost any kind, they always use local landmarks to guide themselves to a gathering-point or a feeding-ground. Even on the stubble field you can make use of this knowledge, discovering that a prominent tree in the hedge is the most likely guide to duck coming in the dusk. If you are proved wrong on one occasion, study the line of approach. It may be that you will discover that another tree, a little higher up or even out in an adjoining field, acts as their steering-mark. Take a position relative to the landmark and you will have a much better chance of getting your duck than simply hoping that one will pass overhead. As you learn about a particular marsh, and prove this for yourself, you will discover the real fascination of fowling lies in acquiring knowledge of the way duck fly and how they come in. As your familiarity with one place increases you will discover that you are developing an eye for certain things, almost an instinctive knowledge of the principal features, so that when you go to a strange place, a marsh with which you have no previous acquaintance, you will know exactly where to stand and the duck will come over you.

I recall applying this instinct on a marsh to which I once went with a friend at the invitation of the owner who sent his regrets at not being able to show us over the place himself. I looked at the flooded ground, the gnarled, lichened trees along one side, the rising ground with the thicket of thorns and scrub oaks on the other, and I made a prediction about the flight, choosing my position without doubting that I might be anything but right. My companion was content to take the other side of the marsh. He could see the duck coming up the side of the thicket and dropping in over his head, but I knew how it would be, just as I always knew when a trout would rise. Darkness closed in upon us. The duck came late but when they came they were exactly where I expected them to be. My com-

panion came off without having had a shot. Very well, he
said, for once I was right, but what about the next time?
We had other opportunities to test my confidence. The
duck never came in from any other direction unless they
were disturbed by heavy shooting. Each time they came
they flew across on my left side. If they were prevented
from dropping in they swung round to the right and
crossed again precisely where they had made their first
approach. Once my companion, seeing them go down in
the middle of the marsh while I was somehow fumbling
with my gear, waded out and flushed them. They flew
off in a widening circle. I was able to shoot the leading bird despite the lowering black clouds that formed the
background.

This kind of thing is marsh lore, something that no one
can teach you unless you have the basic instinct to begin
with. In a little while you begin to see that things seemingly haphazard and without pattern are by no means so.
Instinct in man and beast is strong, and the layers of habit
implanted on the subconscious are the fabric of instinct.
In a flight of duck there is almost always one old bird that
has flown over a place before the flight line is established.
The elimination of birds that make mistakes results in a
strain that behaves in a particular way, flies by night and
not by day, for instance, flies here and not there, takes
certain landmarks as bearings. The man who sits in the
marsh has more to engage his mind than his dreams. The
pattern is before him if he can interpret what he sees.

Knowing the flight line isn't the complete answer, of
course. Duck may come in high and far out or too far up
to be reached. They may only offer a shot when they are
flying out and the fowler will have to know the marsh
even better if he plans to shoot duck coming off. At the
same time, no one can say when duck will leave a marsh.
The urgency of departure is less than the urgency of
arrival because fowl come to the marsh to feed and return

to the open water to roost in nine cases out of ten, but they may leave late in the morning when the fowler is more eager for his breakfast than to watch the sunrise. They may depart with the lingering moon which lies in the clearing morning sky like a silver coin. Flush the birds after they have come in only when you know that they will pass over you or your companion and be sure that you can judge how high they are as they climb up into the darkening sky. A marsh presents problems not encountered on a river or on the stubble. A field has boundaries that are more or less regular. A stubble can be searched by man and dog without too much trouble. A river flows one way or the other, and with some knowledge of its flow and the currents it is often possible to make a reasonable guess as to the coming aground of a bird that drops in the water, but the marsh remains what it is, a black jungle, a huddle of witch-like gorse and broom, stunted trees like dinosaurs or wallowing monsters of the primeval mud, deep holes, underwater obstacles that entangle the unwary, roots and branches and engulfing mud that may take a horse to the ears.

A dog that seeks a fallen duck in the marsh may have a fine nose and yet come struggling back again and again without having anything to show. A duck that falls in a waterhole leaves little scent. When it hits the mud it may hang a moment or two on the surface and then abruptly slip down out of sight. It is hard to tell, considering the possible angles and the visibility, just how far out a fast-flying duck may have arched before it hit the marsh. The search can go on and on without reducing frustration. Anyone who shoots a marsh must be prepared for frustrations, occasionally to suffer in the pursuit of a bedraggled fowl that will almost certainly be regarded at home as a pathetic excuse for getting wet through and bringing back a fair sample of mud and peaty water. Settle in the marsh you will, if you have the makings of a fowler, and you will admit to yourself in due time that the whole business depends on many things, the least important of them being, perhaps, the shooting of a duck, though the duck must occasionally be produced to stay the psychologists or psychiatrists summoned to consider and analyse your state of mind.

Sit in the marsh and think about these things if you must, but never, if you are to continue in your enjoyment, think about them too long or too deeply! It should not be necessary to make an excuse for the experience. You sit listening to the water trickling from one patch of flooded ground to the next, to the rustle of leaves and the small sounds made by lesser marsh birds going to roost in the reeds or the goat-willow close at hand. You see the flighting woodcock seeming as big as a man's hat and the bats that seem to be flying all night. The scents of the marsh are wonderful for they are the scent of honeysuckle, meadowsweet, reeds and rushes, the tangy smell of water-weeds and peat, of marsh gas, the smell of fungus, mildew, moss and lichen. The breeze blows the round rushes, whispers in the broom or gorse and above the sound you hear the wings of duck as they go beating round to the far end beyond the alders. One or two always seem to drop down there first, but the main flight, when it comes, streams in across the rushes, almost touching down, rising for a second and showing the white of their underwing feathers as they alight head-on to you. There never was a moment more full of excitement than this! Hold hard, for many a novice fails because he simply loses his head and shoots like an automaton. Take a breath and hold it, shoot deliberately, smoothly, and be content that you have killed one bird with one stone, without attempting more.

Where to shoot the fast-flying mallard as it goes across your front? The whole world will tell you how far ahead to shoot, and how to do this thing that must in the end become an instinct. I can only tell you what my grandfather told me. It was a very simple thing and I have scratched my head about it ever since. 'Shoot them in the head,' he said, but I am inclined to think that he wasn't giving me the literal answer, or perhaps he didn't think I really needed one. Watch the duck as they go. Put up your gun and never take your eyes off them. Never look at the foresight, never aim. Look at your quarry and shoot —and keep your eyes wide open. If the gun comes to your shoulder as it should, your aim must be right. All that remains doubtful is judgement of range, for the swing you make as you follow the bird and pull the trigger will take care of all the nonsense the theorists have about lead. You may be shooting at birds beyond the range of the gun. Well, better men than you or I have done this a hundred times, and will do it again, but if the gun fits and you obey these rules you are only behind the expert in judgement of distance, always providing you shoot without excitement, the way a good golfer drives a ball. We are not all made of the same stuff and we are not all in search of the same rewards, but marsh shooting, and particularly flighting in the dark, separates the casual rough shooters from the dedicated fowlers. It also tends to eliminate from the company those who simply shoot to kill and have no other excuse for being on a marsh.

It hardly matters to me whether I bag a duck or not, so perhaps I am almost on the way to being qualified to join the Chinese philosopher who first of all removed the barb from his hook so as to avoid inflicting pain on the fish and then finally removed the hook from his line because the biting of the fish interrupted his train of thought! Flighting an Anglesey marsh on the last day of January once, I sat beside a willow tree that was covered in fat golden catkins. It was a cold evening and the light lingered on the flat countryside because the sky was clear of clouds. A moorhen scuttled over my feet. I was sitting still in the shelter of the willow with my legs dangling in the drain,

but the duck refused to come in even when the light died
and the moon began to climb from behind the mountains
in Caernarvonshire. It was my first time on that marsh and
I expected great flights of duck, for I had driven down the
road that bounded it many times at nightfall and had seen
duck dropping in good numbers, lit for a moment or two
by the glare of car headlights. That evening, however,
they didn't come. It was cold and growing colder. It
seemed that the moon was frozen on the sky and the swell
of the fields beyond the marsh appeared to be frost-
covered, even though frost didn't generally appear until
after midnight in that particular place. At last, when my
feet were numb and my hands so cold that I could hardly
feel the gun, duck came. They came from all directions
but so fast and so low that I didn't get a chance to shoot.
I stood up and walked off by a route I had carefully pros-
pected beforehand, but not one duck left the marsh as I
went. The season was at an end the next day. I had sat
looking at the moon, peering through the willow branches,
for maybe three hours—for nothing.

I never got back to that marsh because it changed hands
the following season, but I remember that evening, the
sunset, the twilight, the rising of the moon and at last the
black shapes of the incredibly fast-flying duck sweeping
in, it seemed, frlm all points of the compass. It is framed
in my recollection of evening flights, even if I never fired
a shot, nor needed to put the pull-through down the gun
barrel. There have been other occasions, of course, when
I shot more duck than I needed for my own table and one
or two when I succumbed to an urge to prove my marksmanship and gathered duck I was ashamed to admit I had
shot, but most of the time my expeditions to the marsh
have been moderately rewarding in kind—most rewarding
in experience.

There is one last thing I would warn the would-be
marsh fowler to consider. The marsh lives and breathes.

It has a damp atmosphere. In the days of our grandfathers and great-grandfathers it was said that the night air kills. Indeed, as a boy I was continually warned of the hazards of going out and hanging about in the night air, which didn't mean dallying with country wenches but wandering the burn to fish, or waiting to shoot at flighting duck. Too spartan an individual may get the marsh in his bones. I never believed this when I was a youngster, but I believed very little of the wisdom of my elders at that time. Now, I must admit, the marsh tends to send twinges through my frame. I am not sure whether it is the marsh I know now or rather the marsh I knew thirty or forty years ago, the flood I stood in when I flighted on a drained loch in Scotland, the wet rushes of a bog that knew me in the twilight when the rain was steaming down and even the curlews were silent. A little comfort is not unreasonable, nor does it detract from your manhood. Insulate yourself from the wet log, find somewhere better to dangle your legs than a flowing drain. Carry a flask to warm your stomach when it sorely needs warmth, and go home between evening and morning flight!

7

Tides Run

F R O M their nature fowl are great frequenters of estuaries —broad expanses of sand cut by the river hurrying after the tide, by the very maw of the sea that draws into it the water from a thousand hills and upland pastures. Away out beyond the last bush or tree, the last rock rolled in the icecap, long banks of shingle graduate to tail-ends of gravel and the water, brackish a mile back, is as salt as the sea. Away out here, swimming merrily against the current in the shallows, a duck or two will feed. Farther out a raft of duck may lie at roost like moored craft, all dozing with their necks relaxed, bills on their breasts or turned back across a wing. The estuary is like the very rim-edge of the world, safe from surprise with miles and miles of skyline across which everything comes or goes, the solitary steamer trailing smoke, or a lonely seabird on its private journey from one out-of-sight headland to the next. The tide murmurs and flows to quicksand. The light is bright, and the land far away.

There is no lonelier place for a man to venture, and nowhere can he lose his life more abruptly and vanish without trace. The fowl of the estuary may not know this, but they realize where they are safe. The wigeon or mallard move only when the tide disturbs them. The incoming flood resists the river, holds it behind the sandbank where weeds and leaves slow down and swirl and turn in widening circles. Then the tide in its strength rolls over the mussel-beds, boiling for a while in a froth, and later smooths and rushes all the debris of the river back and back, in reversed waves that rock the roosting wigeon, and there is no comfort left for them.

Duck fly in the twilight, feed at night, roost by day, and roost in places according to the tide, but they move when the flood rocks them and propels them at too fast a pace. They fly from the water and keep to the course of the river except here and there where they can overlook the depressions of the banks ahead, and up they come, a party of two or three followed by four or five, and another one or two, or perhaps a sort of swarm of wigeon all moving away from the rough water to make a half-way journey to their feeding-places on the main stream. The fowler who must learn the business will wait a long time to know all the answers about the flight of duck and their behaviour under particular conditions. The story will be similar to the one unfolded by the study of the marsh. It will take as long to learn.

The old fowler knows that duck will travel in the twilight at their feeding time but he knows much more about their movements on the estuary because he has studied what happens when high tide comes in mid-afternoon or an hour before dusk. He knows, too, that when reaches of the estuary lie uncovered for longer periods at neap tide duck will flight in larger numbers at dusk. The novice may study the ways of all sorts of fowl and profit by it, for the pattern of their behaviour is something he will come to value. A cormorant flies upriver following the tide when shoals of small fish swim in. This is not in itself significant but the small fish feed on all sorts of things that fowl themselves may be taking in the shallower water. The man who watches acquires a feeling for the atmosphere of the estuary and a special knowledge of the significance of things that happen. It may be enough that some casual observer tells the fowler that when he was down recovering a lost mooring or searching for a dinghy that had gone adrift a dozen mallard got up from a particular corner, but personal observation will hold the key to the question of the whereabouts of the same company of duck today and the time when they might again be encountered in that place. The tide and not the clock marks time, the tide, its volume and height, the condition of the river, and the wind and weather in general. With great enthusiasm the eager fowler may hurry off across the bay, his thigh boots leaving tracks on the sand that diffuse and fade almost before he has gone a quarter of a mile. He may stalk the winds of the river with care to come to the place where the duck were seen a day or two before, only to discover that the stretch of water is deserted save for the half-buried post that lies gathering a coating of green weed raked from the tide as it ran.

The journey back can fill the heart with dismay. On a vast expanse of sand or shallow water I once found myself running because I couldn't see a single landmark anywhere, though the day was still clear enough. For minutes on end I lumbered forward, imagination producing a horror that the tide, when it did flow in, would come between me and the land. I forgot the duck. They were farther out. I was still running when they came in past me, but I didn't see them until they were well beyond range again. I had miscalculated and failed to think about the ways of duck as I already knew them. In half an hour, when behind me the tide was beginning to show a line of white, I had exhausted my strength and was incapable of running any more. I plodded on and beat the tide, but I remembered that day. I forget how many duck were out there. I forget what size of flight passed me, but I remember the day, the endlessness of the sand along which I walked looking for signs of duck on the wet banks and the rippling plain ahead of me. It remains a nightmare.

There never was a more dangerous place to wait for duck than the mudbanks of tidal waters that consist of large expanses of shallows when the tide is up, for the man who wades shallows at dusk one evening may be tempted to repeat the shortcut an evening or two later when the passage is even easier and succumb to an urge to attain objectives that can only be reached during a few critical minutes. The tide flows like a snake swimming, smoothly, almost imperceptibly, and the most terrifying thing about it is the way it creeps along depressions and channels not always nearest the main flood. Birds may be seen on sandbanks high and dry and well within the terrain across which the flood will eventually come. Sometimes the fowler might be forgiven for thinking that they settled there to lure him out!

The man who knows the tide looks at his watch. It isn't only a matter of making a simple calculation but of knowing what sort of tide is running. It isn't yesterday the old fowler is thinking about, but the spring tides of a lifetime, the fowling seasons he has known, the way it was in that very spot on a winter's afternoon when he discovered how to escape from drowning. Accidents happen to old and experienced wildfowlers every decade or two, for there is something extraordinary about this kind of tragedy. An ignorant novice drowns because he knows nothing and an old hand drowns because he has become too familiar with danger. More than the relentlessness of the spring tide has to be calculated. An inshore wind fills the creeks faster; the great whales of mud sink sooner than they did the day before, and for once the duck leave early, flighting away up beyond the salt to drop into the reeds and rushes flanking the meadows. Who would die for a duck that tastes of mud? Many a man lost in the rolling torrent could in his last moments answer that question. Man doesn't always die for good reasons, with self-respect and dignity, or half the poor fellows who die on the roads would be spared!

The flow of the water in the estuary when it spreads out to cover so much mud and sand forms a great lake on to which fowl will drop. It would be strange indeed if fowlers stayed within the boundaries of fields and fences and walls and watched the crepuscular movement of their quarry without ever venturing after them, wading waist-deep to gain access to less deep places, taking with them a good dog to retrieve the bag, or paddling out in a rubber boat, a leaky dinghy, a punt, to sit moored on the tide and shoot. This is an ancient pastime, much older than the percussion cap gun or the flint-lock.

Tidal waters are not all fraught with danger to the man who ventures on them after twilight. The secret paths belong to the initiated, the old hands who know where to walk, and how far to go in order to pass an obstruction. The native has his landmarks: a house away on the far shore, a brickworks chimney, a crumbling jetty, a wreck. He looks for these with anxiety when the mist is closing in, and moves, as the wigeon move, because he has become uncomfortable. Time to go, he says, when it seems the night is young and flight after flight of duck go ghosting over the muds, but time to go it is, because the landmarks are becoming indistinct. He won't risk not finding them again in case he ends staring at the sky, spreadeagled on the mud with the tides carrying him in and out until a search party finds him.

Duck fly on fixed lines when they travel the estuary. The lines are almost as well defined as the railway track.

Down in the shelter of a mudbank you are situated directly under the passing duck. They come at intervals and the tide glides on, climbing the bank imperceptibly, completely without sound or warning of any kind. Move when you see the black glaze on the mud and you discover that already you are perched on a treacherous slope. Beyond the hillock there is a frightening sheet of water with enfolding arms about to link. This happens in minutes. When you rush through the water a foothold disintegrates and you are in deep, paddling like a frightened dog, your bag and coat afloat, your cartridges and filling waders dragging you down. The old hand could have told you just when to leave the line, and now, when the water is seemingly staying where it is as though by providential intervention, he could tell you not to head from it but to head into it, and get wet again, for you will soon be forced to swim again unless you do, and swim on and on until you are in danger of losing contact with solid ground altogether.

Every so often an old hand finds himself trapped in the estuary and waits for the tide to finish flowing and begin ebbing again. There are places where they know that this is the best thing to do, but of course no one wants to stand in the tide and wait for hours: even the most hardy of fowlers draws the line at this, except in dire emergency! Wait for the flight by all means, take a stand as near the flight line as you can get, but be sure that you know how you may escape when the tide proves to be higher than expected. Have with you the means of navigating your passage back, a torch, a compass.

The tide runs far up some rivers. I used to hire a boat to go upriver, and either shoot when twilight came, retrieving the duck from the water, or allow myself to be carried back on the slow current to meet duck flying upstream. Flights of wigeon would come to take their supper on the weed-beds. Parties of mallard would converge on the river from lakes on adjoining land, for mallard are fond of flowing water and enjoy short flights at dusk from river to pasture and back again. I loved to sit in the boat while the tide was running and let it carry me to the reeds, an almost soundless voyage save for the occasional movement of the oars to keep the boat heading in the right direction. Mallard would suddenly be there in front of me, in a bay in the reeds, swimming to and fro, feeding or sporting themselves one minute, and the next, splashing into the air with water dripping from their feet and wings. When I shot they would be drawn off the river by the first startled few ascending. For a little while I would pull into the reeds and conceal myself as best I could. It was some-times a long journey for a mallard or two. The tide wasn't always quite suitable and would sometimes still be flooding when I had to return downstream. The rowing was long and tiring. There were difficulties that sometimes reduced me to a point where my enthusiasm vanished, especially when I had to row and bale, and the tide seemed to be carrying me two yards back for every yard I managed to propel the boat forward, or when a duck, dropping in the deep water, floated and spun away from me because I hadn't gained enough distance to pick it up.

There was one night in particular when I lost an oar and watched it drifting upwater. The tide was powerful. I could do nothing but dip the gun butt into the water and use it as a substitute oar, which I did, but it was a long time before the badly balanced boat came up with the 'swimming' oar and I was able to snatch it back again. Duck flew up and down past me, aware, it seemed to me, that I was in no position to do anything about it. That night the ebb was late and I had to row down in the dark. The one duck I brought down fell in the depths of the reeds where I could neither reach it by wading nor spoon it out with the oar. I had no dog. There is surely a moral in that!

The estuary isn't a place of danger and horror un-
relieved by any redeeming feature. There is a special
beauty that those who love to shoot there know well, a
beauty at evening and morning that makes the day between
seem dull and of no importance, a beauty I knew once at
the mouth of a small river running into the Solway. It was
a morning of mist that trailed on the river. Every ten
minutes or so the air would be rent by the coming of a
pair of teal on their way back from their feeding-ground.
On the mud waders were talking to each other as they do
at first light. An oyster-catcher paraded in front of me. I
was waiting for mallard to come over from the marsh. They
always crossed this minor estuary on their way. They
didn't come, but I was fascinated by the unexpected teal,
none of which I was able to aim at because they came so
low, so fast, that they were upon me and away again before
I gathered my wits. The sun was spreading a gold radiance
over the whole of the eastern sky above the mist and the
mist itself produced a sort of mirage effect on tall elm trees
back behind the marsh pasture. The trees looked at least
a hundred and fifty feet high. A whitewashed farm beneath
them was a blurred huddle of stonework but its slate roofs
appeared high and steep. Away above it all, geese, and
not my mallard, flew out of the Solway muds, in long,
wavering lines, talking happily to one another, the sound
spreading far and wide across the sleepy countryside. The
mist cleared. Near at hand things lost their glamour.
Fences acquired shadows. Grass hanging on bushes and
spars of gates in places where there had been a flood tide
turned from grey to gold in the morning sun. I had made
my way down in complete darkness, following a railing,
a creek and then some humps of eroded bank the tide had
at one time or other transported down the estuary. The
tide had long since run out. I could see it on the sand's
edge, perhaps half a mile away, perhaps more, for who can
judge distance in a place like that? I didn't shoot anything

at all that morning but I remembered it and the geese, and the startling suddenness of the teal.

By contrast there was an evening on another estuary a hundred miles away when I took my stand behind a large boulder, a rock big enough to shelter two men, and watched the evening sun take fire, blaze for perhaps an hour, and then sink to a glimmer like a peat fire dying in the grate. We were waiting for duck to come up from the sea. They came, wave after wave of them, hundreds of wigeon hurrying to feed. There never was such a sight for they were all black as night against the sky, rushing along, swerving, swinging and whistling in the manner of wigeon. The sand was wet and almost clear of debris or driftwood. Here and there a sunken stone lay protruding from the smooth surface. I noticed them for what they were when I went out to recover the duck we shot. I remember standing there with a brace of wigeon, their heads securely held in between my fingers, when another 'invasion' of duck began. I had never seen so many. I didn't run to cover but stood and let them pass. My companion had what he needed for his dinner. He, too, stood and admired the flight while the light died completely, and afterwards we could hear the stragglers passing, an odd one whistling as it went.

8

Moonlight Madness

T H E flighting moon is for those who are ready to stay out of bed. The same sort of man will dally all night by the river waiting for the sea-trout to move, although he will shun the clear, silvery light in which duck can be easily seen. The problem of the moonlight is to know when the duck will come, and to maintain enthusiasm when nothing happens. The moonlit countryside has a kind of old print quality, an immobility that always makes me think of tinted engravings I was given to look through as a small child, for they depicted the hunter's world in which fierce-looking hounds stood like statues in beds of reeds, gazing skywards as duck took flight, and bearded men with strange and unfamiliar guns fired at the escaping fowl. The engravings were by a Russian, I think, and the fowl were those of some Black Sea or Caucasian marsh. It probably wasn't the artist's intention to convey moonlight at all, but moonlight they always were for me, and always are when I think of them as I stand in the night watching for duck going over.

The uncanniness of a still night with wisps of cloud across the heavens is heightened when duck fly high for they seem to travel noiselessly. The whole atmosphere is of a sort of dream-world, in which one's original purpose is lost and time is no more. Far away a dog barks, but its barking becomes a rhythm. An owl sails out across a silvery field but the small cry it makes detracts not at all from the hypnotic effect, the impression of silence and everything at a standstill, no longer harsh in outline, grim or soiled. This can happen in the small hours unless the increasing cold gnaws at one's ears and hands and the chill of the earth penetrates through the soles of one's boots, the gun becomes heavy, timelessness becomes no longer enchanting, and one listens for the church clock. The duck may come or never appear: on the barley field it is always so. Standing in the frozen hedge, the fowler sees a rime on the gate, a haze on the stubble, and wonders if it is past the hour when duck arrived the night before. The world sleeps. If duck haven't come over it is hard to think that they are still afloat on the lake, riding the gentle ripple, unable to make up their minds when to go for their undisturbed night feed, for most of their enemies are only abroad by day. This is often the time when the flight takes place in an unwary moment or two when the fowler tucks his chin into his collar, slips his hands into his pocket, warms his nose with his own breath and thinks of the sensuous comfort of a soft bed and an eiderdown. All duck are black by the light of the moon, all sounds that break the stillness of the night more devastatingly loud. Fire a gun in the heart of the silent marsh at midnight and it seems that the world has burst apart. It is even worse by moonlight. The sound fills one's head. The world jumps and misses a heartbeat, a minute later there is a heavy thud of the duck striking the earth. Time is meaningless until this happens but then the world is changed. Duck are away up in the silver bowl, growing smaller, blurring as they seem to converge or cross each other's trails. Out on the frosted pasture lies the victim, an upturned wing marking its location, a few feathers drifting. It was for this that you came and sat by the gorse bush and began to dream. Now that it is done perhaps you will begin another vigil or slowly make your way home, depending on whether you are a hunter or a poet, a romantic, a moon-struck skygazer who sees nothing odd in sitting in a hedge when hard-working, ordinary men are sleeping to recover from their daily toil.

It is different down on the shore. The wigeon travel as the mood takes them, in to the river to the trailing grass and the weed, out across the sand of the bay, where the tide is no more than a gentle hushing sound, a sigh, and all the seabirds are silent for once while streams and ditches with outlets through the shingle run low. Wigeon by the light of the moon are an artist's dream. The fowler is less inclined to dream of them in the air as in the roasting tin. The little fat wigeon takes a lot of beating when it lies, done to a turn, crisp and brown on the dish!

Shoot in the moonlight and you may have difficulty in being sure of the range, for moonlight is deceiving. The duck that seem to be no smaller than they should prove to be out of range. When this happens the die is cast for me. Judgement of the size and range on the flighting duck hardly ever comes back to me. I might as well go home. When I discover the range at the outset my eye is in, as they say, and I can shoot with the next fellow.

Wigeon are third on my list of duck. I prefer the less greasy mallard, but best of all I like the teal, though they are difficult enough to shoot in all circumstances without the complication of judging their size for range by moonlight with no other sort of duck present for comparison. The problem becomes more acute on the shore and the

sand dunes. Wigeon often come low and fast to the rivermouth. How far is the shingle bed that breaks the flow
of the river? How big is a cock wigeon coming at top
speed off the sea at say thirty yards? This kind of thing
cannot be imparted to the man who comes to shoot by
moonlight for the first time, nor can he be sure that he
has the answer before he knows the problem.

I remember going to wait for wigeon by the light of a
moon on a night in the very early days of the war. My
companion was an old and experienced fowler who knew
the rivermouth and the muds as I could never know them.
He was, moreover, a much better shot than I was. We
took our places as the moon was coming up across the bay,
leaving fifty or sixty yards between us and hoping that
the duck would split the difference. The moon came
slowly. I remember thinking that perhaps we had arrived
too late and the wigeon were already off the tide, but my
companion was quite sure they hadn't come. For one
thing the tide was later, and for another the moon was
almost full. Full moon resulted in the duck changing the
regular pattern of their flight. It gave them a visibility
latitude which on dull and dark nights they couldn't enjoy,
so, no matter what I thought or feared, if I held my tongue
and waited patiently, they would come through. We were
early, considering the conditions. Let the moon climb a
little from the back of the hills. I could not do otherwise.
The moon came up, silhouetting the crags and the higher
mounds, and then, at last, drenching the whole of the bay
in soft light so that I could see pools on the far shore. I
could hear waders in depressions I couldn't see. The
woods on the slopes behind me were touched with silver
but the shadows were blacker, as though the trees stood
in dyed cotton wool. A long way away a train came through
the hills. Nearer at hand a lorry went rattling along a
rough road with a load of empty milk-churns.

I was dreaming when the wigeon came, but not for

long. I shot more than my share. We had a market for them. People were concerned about rations and rationing. I could hear my companion firing furiously in the time the flight lasted. He was still firing at the higher up tail-end of the flight when I had used almost all of my cart-ridges. He joined me on the mud when I was picking up my bag, but he had no wigeon. I couldn't understand it. The wigeon had been just that little bit out of range, just that yard or two in my favour as they tracked overhead to the river.

'I wasn't on to begin with. I never managed to get on,' said my companion.

I found this hard to believe but when I went to stand by the rock my companion had chosen I understood. He was much lower down than I had been. The wigeon had favoured my side. The angle had been in their favour so far as my companion's shots were concerned. To tell the truth I was rather proud of myself until a solitary duck came while I was standing there and when I tried to stop it I completely failed to do so. The wigeon flew as strongly and as determinedly as ever and I could see the light on its wings as it turned a bend in the river's course and dis-appeared. Even an old hand can be deceived in the moon-light, and I should have known better. This wasn't my first outing.

Once I walked our bog in the moonlight thinking to shoot whatever fowl I flushed. The bog was actually three parts of a field that at one time had been completely cultivated. A burn had broken its banks and short-cut a route to the ditch on the far side, slowly isolating the lower part of the field, winter after winter, converting the lower field into a swamp area where little hills of gorse and old stone heaps made islands. The remainder of the field, the higher quarter, was still cultivated and supported a rotation crop of corn and roots with one section, about an acre or so, planted with potatoes.

It was possible to walk the wet side of the bog from the old stubble, flushing duck that fed in the swamp of grass and rushes down below. I had done this a few times on wet days, but never in twilight because it seemed to me that to venture into the rushes when it was too dark to see was inviting disaster. I considered the full moon a perfect time to try my luck and down I went after supper. The bog had its quota of duck. I could hear them and see them occasionally as they came skimming over from the adjoining farms. In a little while, choosing my steps carefully, I was making my way out to them and they rose as though I had been beating the place, one or two going off, and then, as I advanced, one or two more. I shot two after I had flushed two or three dozen and the two I brought down were impossible to recover for the moonlight on the rushes, the bushes and stone heaps lit the place perfectly without removing the lower shadows or making the fallen duck conspicuous. The thought that I would be safer by moonlight proved a delusion. Bog and hard ground looked alike. Soon I was wallowing up to my thighs in a morass of broken turf and black, waterlogged earth. I looked back at the stubble hill, the moonlit ridges of the potato furrows and wished I had never left them! No one was within earshot. The steading was out of sight beyond the stubble and the next pasture and, even so, the lights would be out. Everyone else went to bed after supper. The collie dog was lying under the kitchen table and I was a victim of my own madness. One doesn't die of despair unless despair is complete. I wallowed my way forward, turned over and rolled myself out of the mud, squelched and stumbled and panted and grunted until I was out of breath. In the end I got back to solid ground.

I can smile at the thought of how I must have looked going slowly up over the stubble field like something moulded in black peat. I still had my gun, but it was choked with mud. My clothes were fixed to my body and my hat had gone. It was some distance to the steading and when I got there I didn't know what to do. I could hardly stamp my way into the spotless, scrubbed kitchen in such a state. I put down the gun at the door and stood for a minute or two, wretched and sorry for myself; a madman, if ever there was one, bathed in moonlight, plastered in black earth. Then I began to undress, discarding my jacket, boots, socks, trousers, underclothes. I was as naked, if a little blacker, as the day I was born and I was still not fit to venture across the threshold. I walked down to the pump and gently worked the handle until the water ran, and, with my teeth chattering, I washed myself all over. The only marks on the floor were the wet prints of my bare feet. It didn't take long to encourage the fire to burn. There were peats to hand but all I could discover to dry myself was a hessian hand towel. It was rough and not very large.

The incident might have passed without comment had I not forgotten to clear away my discarded clothes which littered the steps down to the pump. In the morning everyone commiserated with me except my grandfather. He knew the height of my folly. He felt that I had received a lesson about shooting duck by moonlight. I recovered the duck during the day or, to be exact, the dog got them out for me. A bullock could hardly have made a muddier wallow in escaping from the bog than I had done and I never attempted such a thing again.

Most of my moonlight vigils have been in company with other fanatic fowlers, because, much as I enjoy my own company on the river or marsh, there is safety in numbers. The lingering moon lights the return of duck to a favourite roost on a lake and this becomes something like trying a new sort of fly for a trout, although one knows that most innovations fall short of the rosiest dreams. I flighted the morning duck on a certain lake whenever the calendar showed that the full moon would

light the morning sky and did so for as many flights as
circumstances permitted. Duck would come in over the
trees to drop down on to the water at daybreak or a little
after on every-day occasions, but when the moon was up,
I discovered, they came back earlier and less warily, flying
lower over the trees by the light of the moon than they
would by the first light of day. At the same time woodcock
passed from one planting to another and other nocturnal
birds made more frequent journeys.

The difficulty, when the moon was high, was to know
the best stand to take. The duck had not all gone to the
same feeding-place and although they would leave by
more or less the same route they didn't always come in the
same way. Standing among the bankside trees we would
debate the numbers of duck we had heard dropping on
the water after flights had come from unexpected angles,
and the height at which they were coming when small
flights passed to left or right beyond our reach. I always
felt that an upturned face looked whiter by moonlight
than it did in twilight. Now and again we brought duck
down and they crashed far out in the water, sometimes so
far that the dog had to be excused the effort of swimming
such a distance in such icy water.

The experience added to my knowledge of what not to
do. Don't expect to shoot well or, except in the most favourable of conditions, to make a large bag of duck in the
moonlight. Don't go headlong after a wounded bird and
allow yourself to be misled by the light which can disguise
or hide the most dangerous obstacles in your path. Don't
judge a pool's depth by the reflection. Always judge the
bird to be farther up than you think it is, for shooting at
duck that are far out is wasteful but, worse than being
extravagant, it is cruel. Duck die of many things. It is said
that large numbers are done to death by shot that they
swallow when it has fallen into the water to sink among
the weeds and mud, but the most miserable and saddest

death that can be inflicted on anything is the slow, lingering one brought about by irresponsible shooting.

Should the apprentice go out by moonlight? Duck and geese are not classed as game, but snipe and woodcock are, and if by moonlight he should shoot the latter he might find himself debating his right to be called a lawful fowler. The Night Poaching Act, framed in 1828, will be brought out to deal with him. It may be that while he is crossing land in order to reach the marsh or the shore some worthy constable will step out of the shadows to make an arrest. The old act defines trespass with a gun after dark. After dark means after nightfall and the rise of the moon. Fowlers have always shot by moonlight when they had a fancy to do so. Let the novice decide for himself what hazards he is prepared to face and let him shoot by the moon if he has a mind to. If he doesn't, he will miss an experience that he shouldn't be without. He will miss knowing what his hunting ancestors knew, the wonder of the flight under the moon, the flight of duck, and sometimes of geese, for geese, too, move by moonlight and graze the inland meadows, travelling from the estuary to do so. There is an atmosphere that only the fowler knows when he stands by the moonlit pool, waits on the estuary for the duck that make journeys in the dead of night. I and hundreds of others like me have done these things and would not have missed them, whatever scornful lie-abeds have to say about us!

9

Frost and Flood

W H E N the cold wind whispers in the reeds it may not reach the sheltering fowl in the water down below, but a steady fall in temperature puts a layer of ice on the pond or flash, stiffens the mud in open places and drives the duck to feed where it might otherwise never be seen. It is saddening to see the ultimate false tameness induced by conservation of energy and a lowering of vitality. When it is well nourished the duck springs from the water and climbs into the sky with power, skims down over the lake, makes a circuit and comes back in again all in a few seconds or at the most a minute or two, but as the hard weather continues the bird's survival begins to depend on the minimum exertion. It is slow to rise, sluggish on the wing, a prey to the sharpened fox, the falcon, the crow, the big black-backed gulls that wait about like under-takers. It is a cruel world and predation is never governed by a balancing compassion. There is no compassion in the ravenous hunting fox, or the hang-about carrion, for neither would have lived a day with such a handicap. Few men haunt the marsh in hard times. This is not entirely due to the fact that most have pity for the fowl starving on the ice but often simply because a starving waterbird has hardly a picking of meat upon it.

Between the extremes of mild conditions and the iron grip of ice and snow the fowl have more than a slight advantage over the fowler. As frost sets in the balance begins to change. Sometimes when it snows and the snow lies for a day or two the alteration in the habit and habitat of fowl excites the fowler. It happens that a particular corner of a small field remains sheltered. The ground doesn't freeze as hard for some reason or water bubbles from the deep spring and keeps flowing, though elsewhere the ice builds and rime grows on twigs and branches. In some uncanny way fowl of all kinds discover these places. All at once snipe are puddling through the cold wet mud and a single duck or a pair of duck come quite fearlessly gliding down to alight there. The fowler watching the faraway skeins of geese, the passing curlews or migrating plovers, catches his breath. Who can tell about anything when suddenly, in the clear bright light of a cold day, duck come in? No one has all the answers, it seems. There is no final and complete rule. Instinct is in every living creature. Experience is never complete and absolute, especially when it concerns fowl that have built-in mechanisms that tell them here, in this hidden-away corner, things are not what the thermometer or the barometer might indicate to the fowler, and the nature of the land varies not so much because of its topography or salient landmarks but because of something subtle and indefinable.

Every fowler discovers that he can rely upon no invariable law when the weather begins to change from mild to cold. I remember sallying forth with the gun one day at noon because it had stopped snowing and the sight of so many birds heading west to the milder places along the seaboard or on the far side of the sea itself, tempted me to take a walk to see what was happening along familiar streams, in hollows I knew well, flashes I had often visited in more congenial circumstances. Along the first ditch I came to I was startled by the rising of a duck. It was down again before the little trickle of powder smoke had gone from the muzzle of my gun. I lumbered over the snow to retrieve it from where it had dropped behind a hedge and discovered that it wasn't a mallard but a wigeon, though what a wigeon was doing in such a corner I couldn't imagine. There had never been one there before in my experience. It wasn't a solitary bird for a second took wing as I was picking the first and then my walk took its more or less normal course. I flushed a hare and later on common snipe and jacksnipe and a woodcock from a depression beneath an oak tree, a bird that rose in a flurry of snow and shortly afterwards lay on the white background of a drift as though it had been painted on a white board. The wigeon marked that day in my memory. I didn't need to make an entry in my diary, nor did I need to take a photograph of my bag as a memento of the occasion, though I did so. There were no wigeon where I found those two. There never had been and there never would be again or could I say anything with such conviction after that particular experience?

The day had yet to come when I would stand and watch whitefront geese rising from a pond hardly big enough to contain them or see them take off from a place surrounded by virgin snow, but one time I remember them flying unsaluted by fire, beating out through the trees with that lack of haste that characterizes big, powerful birds that cover a considerable distance with what seems to be an effortless and almost lazy wingbeat. Damn! I said to myself as I watched them go. How I tormented myself with thoughts of what I might have done as I stood and gaped until the geese were perhaps a quarter of a mile up in front of me, their wingbeats no longer audible, their shape and colouring indistinct.

There was another day when the ploughed field was covered in snow that blew like a desert duststorm as a light breeze ran across the land. All at once a long flight of greylags came at hedge height right over my head. Again I did nothing, not from compassion, though I could see every small detail of the geese, their eyes, their tucked-away feet, the upcurve of their pinions as they passed over me, as though in some slow-motion film, but from nothing more than sheer paralysis of mind and body. Away they went, at the same height, across the open field in which I stood like a scarecrow, looking along their backs, ex-periencing, for a brief second or two, something I could hardly hope to experience again in a lifetime. I am glad now that I didn't put up the gun and look along it to shoot the geese as they flew innocently onwards. I could have done. I could have done two or three times over. I lived it all again and again afterwards, but I am glad that it never happened. They say that unconsummated love is the only lasting romance. I might have remembered the easy slaughter for the rest of my days or I might have forgotten it, but I should have missed an excitement, the dream that is as vivid now as it was that night when the countryside was blanketed with snow and long, thick icicles were hanging from the rainspout.

Happiness is measured by contrast with a state of misery and success by the degree of one's previous failure, or the failures of others, but I am ready to admit that my enjoyment in retrospect springs as much from occasions when I failed, or was unable to shoot, as from shooting and bringing down the thing at which I aimed. If you are to understand the pure joy of fowling I believe that the experience in itself comes above the tangible result. Although one may take a pride in bringing down a duck

or a goose there is so much more to it all than those who
kill for killing's sake or bird-watch for bird-watching's
sake can hope to understand.

Once, on a long-ago morning, before I had a gun of
any sort, the snow came and stayed to build up between
the drystone walls and the ricks in the rickyard until it
was hard to define roads, fields or rickyards and hedges
around them. I remember it so well because the snow-
buntings were in the rickyard for days before this happened and all at once the buntings, too, had gone, hurrying across the snow-smoothed fields after flights of finches,
starlings and other migrating birds. That morning the
geese came in hundreds, disorientated by the snow-flurries,
the lack of landmarks on land they knew well. We stood
at the door watching them when it seemed that they
would hit the roof, for roof and field and hills beyond were
all of a white blend. There was a gun standing in the
corner by the grandfather clock, and cartridges too,
enough to bring down all the geese anyone could ever
have wanted. It was the habit in our household to snatch
up that gun if a hare offered himself on the field beyond
the kitchen window or a covey of partridges sailed over
the wall in the pigs' field, but no one ran for it. No shot
was fired. I was puzzled. I remember asking afterwards
why the greylags were allowed to pass so close to the door
without one being brought down, and being told that the
poor things had wandered, lost like the wethers out on
the hill, the old horse away down in the grim landscape
of the bog where the rushes were buried and the old,
lightning-struck ash tree stood gaunt and bare.

There is a time when one may hold one's hand or a
certain paralysis will prevent the gun going up, and no
one makes excuses when this happens. My great-great-
grandmother, who was a witch, would have said that
'spellbound' is no mere figure of speech!

What I have written is not to persuade the newly

initiated fowler to refrain from shooting when the weather is cold or snow comes, for this he will do in due course according to his conscience, just as he will sensibly take advantage of conditions that are temporarily in his favour without afterwards regarding himself as having been unsportsmanlike. In general wildfowl are a great deal better equipped to take care of themselves than most people give them credit for. They move as a rule long before they are starved and weak, for they are highly sensitive to changes in weather and their movements are often taken as reliable indication of change even when the weather forecasters are busy hedging their bets. In flood conditions, of course, fowl are far from vulnerable. They moor themselves on the great sea of the flooded meadows and sit there throughout the day while swans paddle their way through the sluggish flow of brown water, plovers retreat on the muddy plough, and coots and waterhens seek the tops of rush beds that are slowly vanishing in the rising water.

The fowler stands away back on the high ground and tries to make an assessment of the situation, admiring the rafts of duck that dot the meadows between the disappearing hedges. If only a man could get out there and shoot where the willows mark the river's course! If only the fowl were not so wary! Wariness is proportionate to the danger of being stalked. The duck on the flood can see acres and acres of water and all the fields that fall to the river. It is an impossible situation unless one has a boat, a punt or a rubber dinghy with which to negotiate the flooded fields and paddle to the shelter of the hedges protruding from the water. Fools venture and forget the depth and width of streams and ditches and sometimes the state of boggy ground barely covered by the flood once the water has penetrated to turn it into quagmire. The duck watch the adventurous fowler as he struggles out towards them, and then away they go, half a mile upriver, to settle again. Flood may fascinate but it also frightens me and time and again, before I had accumulated my years, flood plucked at my coat!

There was a day just before the war when I went to shoot an inland marsh in late October. It had been raining steadily for several days and the planks that bridged the burn draining the marsh were almost awash. The peaty water crept over them in places. The little bridges skimmed the debris of the flood until the force of the current spread it over the planks and away it sped downstream. I remember winding my way into this place and watching the lowering cloud that simply poured rain upon it and never thinking about the road back. Duck were going to and fro, screened by the cloud and the steady downpour. I knew where I had to go. I had my favourite place in the shelter of a great straggling willow with a score of branches rising directly from the water as though they belonged not to one but a dozen trees. I found my place and settled there. Every half-hour or so I disturbed the marsh with the report of my gun and its echoes. The rain speared into the pools all round me. In a little while I had moved until I could move no farther and still keep the water below the tops of my wellingtons, so I resigned myself to being waterlogged. I was gathering one or two mallard and enjoying being there in the private world of the marsh and the flighting fowl, a place that sheltered deer in its more remote clearings, deer and tall, sturdy bog hares.

It was almost dark before I left. I couldn't hope to retrieve duck in such a flood in the dark. I was content to go. The exhilaration of shooting and being there had begun to pall when the rain got through to my shoulders and finally ran in a cold rivulet down between my shoulder blades. I floundered back along the path but the burn was no more! It had disappeared in the flood and with it the slippery planks. The planks were below the water for they were all bedded and secured in stones but how could I hope to find them? I cast about for outlying landmarks, tied my bag of duck to my oilskin coat, gripped the gun and waded out into the thickening gloom of nightfall. It wasn't surprising that I failed to find the plank at the first attempt. The burn engulfed me. My hat swam away so fast that I lost sight of it before I had half-turned to look where it had gone, but I came up on the bank and struggled to stand. My knees were barked on hidden rocks and I knew how much colder the burn was than the rain that fell from the clouds. At the second attempt I found the plank. It was no more than chance that guided my foot to it. I took short steps and held myself firm against the flood. Crossing seemed to take a long time but once on the far side I hurried down the line of the bank to the next plank for the way swung first to one side and then to the other. Twice I almost misjudged the course of the burn but saved myself and at last found the second bridge. It was almost completely dark when I reached solid ground and the road and when I did so I could hear duck passing right overhead. A horse had fallen into the burn only the day before and had been swept to its death. I didn't know about that, of course, or my nerve might have failed me. There are fowl where there is flood, but it isn't always very wise to pursue them quite so far.

An acquaintance made the mistake of doing what I did on an estuary he thought he knew well, crossing over to get at wigeon that had settled close in when the tide was about to turn. The wigeon were a little beyond his reach, but he is a man of philosophical outlook and he was content to wait. In due course the duck came closer yet and he shot to his heart's content, although he had to resign himself to the thought that some of the duck he had put down had gone sailing upriver and would be picked out by the predatory villagers half a mile inland. The flood that was on the way down wasn't enough to stop the dead duck floating in, but its effect was to deepen the crossing.

No faint heart by any stretch of imagination, the gentle-
man in question strode boldly into the current but when
the undertow lifted him and deposited him again a few
yards farther on, dipping him in the water without giving
him time to close his mouth, he decided that he would
have to stand his ground and trust to luck, or risk being
wafted away by the flood. The water rose steadily, filling
the cavities in his already saturated clothing, reaching up
to his chest, his collarbone, his chin. He held the gun in
the air, not knowing what to do next but swim for his life
without great hope of coming out, but it seemed that the
water was reluctant to come that last inch or two. It stayed
where it was. It stayed where it was for a long time and
then, slowly, it went down again. In the course of this
falling of the tide a man came down the opposite bank
and looked anxiously across the flood. My friend made no
sound. He was cold and wretched, but proud. What would
the world say if it discovered him there with his arms in
the air, motionless as a cormorant drying itself out and
whimpering to be rescued? No, he couldn't ask for help.
In time he would wade across and make his way home to
a hot bath and bed. This is what he did. The water fell.
He walked across the riverbed and saved himself but the
world knew about it. There was an alarm for a lost fowler
on the marsh. Police with grappling irons and powerful
torches were there, to say nothing of men with boats and
lifebelts and lifejackets, and at least one villager holding
two dead wigeon.

'I was perfectly safe,' said the flood victim. 'Never in
any danger at all, and I'll thank you for the wigeon. I shot
them and would have had them out but for the tide.'

And he took the wigeon and went home, but never
again did he go across the estuary when the river was in
flood.

10

Teal Flight

NEXT to the way they spring almost vertically into the air the most impressive thing about the little teal, the smallest duck, is the furious rush of their arrival. Teal always seem to hurry, coming through the morning mist or the twilight like a train, startling anyone who waits in the reeds or rushes. They come in haste and they depart in haste and when they drop they are down quite abruptly. It isn't always possible to flush them again by clapping one's hands, and if one does it may happen that the teal are away before the gun can be picked up and brought to bear upon them. They come in pairs most of the time and they are the fastest duck on the wing. They are also the neatest things on a platter and by far the tastiest. I would rather wait for a teal flight than any other sort of duck but places where teal come in numbers are rare and hard to discover, and no one who has only seen odd pairs of teal flighting when mallard are on the move can understand how much more exciting the scene is when the teal are coming in close. There may be some old word for the flight of teal. To me they might be called a bombardment. There is no other description that fits so well, especially if one is well hidden at the very centre of the flighting place.

Teal, say the experts, are the test of the fowler's marksmanship—discounting, of course, the elusive snipe which has far too much space around it—and the experts are not to be denied. When the teal is flushed from the weedy stream, it rises almost vertically, climbing the thorn hedge and rushing away once it has gained height. There is time to consider the teal after the opportunity to shoot has gone, for often it swings round in the sky and goes away high overhead, a miniature duck speeding across the countryside with its mate in tow. Who wouldn't pause to watch and wonder about the ways of the diminutive duck: the handsome little cock birds with their vermiculated feathers so coveted by fly-tiers, the brown little hens, dowdy partners for such smart mates! The teal search the banks of the stream and swim quietly along the fringes of the pools, two of them in company more often than not, and as unobtrusive as the bank-vole or the water-shrew as they go. Few blundering fowlers ever get a chance to see them when they aren't nervous and alert; but when the stream is at peace and the countryside all about quiet and undisturbed the teal are like small replicas of some domestic breed of fowl belonging to a Lilliputian world, places where the mace is a hundred feet high and the thorn trees are part of an equatorial forest, they are so far above the ground and the bays and backwaters of the stream.

Let the fowler who would dine on teal walk with caution and learn to know the place for them, for often this is what he will depend upon, a knowledge of the sort of stream, waterhole, pond or overgrown flash in the corner of which a brace of teal will be feeding or sheltering on a not too cold winter's afternoon. The ditches and feeder streams are always more sheltered and free from frost than the open water, the lake or the river, and teal love the gravelly shallows, the rippling weed-beds through which the clear clean water flows, the places where the smell of mint may be delicate and watercress abound just beyond the mud where the cattle drink. Step cautiously and think only about the little duck as you would think of the woodcock in the hazel copse while you cross the compacted bed of dead leaves. The teal will rise without a second's warning, stopping your heartbeat, it will seem; freezing you in an immobility to rival the pointing dog. Along this same stream in another corner you may get a second chance, for a haunt of teal has characteristics that bring the little duck in from miles around. Walk on and walk carefully. The teal hear you coming. They swim a little way and take cover, perhaps below an overhanging bush, screened from you by a branch or two that spans the water, and you will only see them when they are in the air, a second or two before it is too late, before they are almost out of danger.

It is as exciting to be outwitted by teal as it is to shoot them, so far as I am concerned. One minute they are there, and the next they are sweeping across the open field, contouring the hill perhaps fifty or sixty yards above it, and going fast. A man who really appreciates this can laugh at his failure. There is no shame in being made a fool. Most of us, the most crafty stalkers or hunters, were born foolish. The advantage is with the smart little duck that has such climbing power to assist it into the sky. The way they go has to be admired. The unexpectedness of their flight is one of the greatest natural delights a fowler can experience.

Teal find feeding-places by prospecting for them, flying in and out of the area in which they may roost to search the farmland, the waterholes, the ponds hardly big enough to please a moorhen, away in some low corner of the cattle pasture, the lush-grown banks of the bigger ditches, places where the water washes the gravel as though to expose fragments of gold in the finest grit. Here and there in hard weather, they converge on a marsh and make it their own, a place with stunted trees, old drunken fences and few solid paths capable of providing passage for anything bigger than a hare or anything heavier than a sheep. Out among the rushes the teal will search for food and work their way from waterhole to waterhole, arriving at dusk and departing at morning in the manner of duck. The man who knows of such a place can hardly be blamed for keeping the information to himself. Haunts of teal are not used for very long when they are flighted heavily by more guns than the area can properly accommodate. When you discover a teal marsh, give thanks. When you find a stream where teal are to be flushed mark it well, for there, in similar conditions at about the same time of year, you will come upon the little duck again.

One such marsh I knew well. It was not more than a mile from the sea, but sheltered from the cold north-easterly wind by a hillock. On the southern and western sides the marsh was similarly protected. The fields about it were old, scrub-grown pastures with lank grass. They were divided by crumbling drystone walls topped with blackberry tangles, strands of sagging barbed wire, an occasional blackthorn standing like a crone above it all waving arms and casting a spell on that lonely tract of rushes and willows where the teal came when the weather was at its coldest. I discovered the place by accident, standing one wintry afternoon to watch a barn owl perched on an old oak post on the fringe of the rushes. He balanced against the wind and spread his wings to do so without taking off or seeming to want to. I thought that soon he would drop down into the boggy ground in front of him and come up with a vole or a mouse, for I was sure that he was hunting and not simply exercising his wings. The performance went on but I never discovered what it was about for all at once a teal came sweeping over, braked in the air and literally plunged into the rushes. A moment later a second little duck did the same. I was excited, but I knew that with all the intervening marsh to cross with waterholes and heaving mats of lying grass I could not hope to come up with the teal. I stood where I was, turning my attention once again to the balancing owl, but I had hardly done so when two, four, six teal rushed in. In half an hour I counted between thirty and forty. I could hardly believe what I had seen. Surely, it seemed to me, these were teal in the process of migrating across the country? I walked to the edge of the marsh and they began to spring out of the rushes, a startling, dramatic sight as they departed like snipe but with more disturbance. Tomorrow, I told myself, I would be back to check the place again. I departed without firing a shot. The following afternoon I took a stand among the willows. The flight began at the same time and in the same way, two, four, six and then teal I couldn't count because they came when it was almost dark and dropped in everywhere except within range of my hiding-place. I wasn't dismayed. This, after all, is what flighting is, the choice of place, patience, an experience to be enjoyed whether one shoots or not.

It wasn't the same on the third occasion for I had considered the marsh and the area in which the small duck were settling. There was no cover except for a low, creeping bush. I waded out to it and was delighted to find that it was growing on a small island of stones, an area of about two feet by four, big enough to allow me to sit and wait in comfort, although if I didn't lie down I was bound to be too conspicuous. I had to lie down, then. The bush would give me cover if I elbowed my way into it and trusted that I hadn't hidden myself like an ostrich hiding itself in the open by sticking its head in a small hole. I managed to insinuate my body into the thorn bush. My legs dangled in the waterhole adjoining the stones, but at least they were screened by rushes. Holding the gun was a problem. I could hold it well enough but not in a position that would allow me to shoot. Time enough for that when the teal were dropping in, I told myself as I began the long vigil. Settling in, I watched small birds crossing and recrossing the marsh. I heard a cock pheasant that seemed to be only a few yards from me, but in the direction in which my heels were pointing. The pheasant clucked and crowed his way to roost and peewits wheeled overhead and skimmed in above the rushes, filling the air with the sound of their aerobatics as they dived and turned and dived. Far off I could hear a dog barking and the heavy thud of a cottage door being slammed.

It was dusk. The teal came at last. Perversely they dropped behind me, to my left and right, before the first splashed into a pool not four yards from me and departed almost at once because the sound of the gun being drawn quickly through the thorn bush must have sounded like the approach of a cat or a fox. I reared up, the thorns lacing my hands, and swung round to shoot at the duck I disturbed but I couldn't get on to one of them, and away they went in the gloom. A minute or two later they, or perhaps a new flight of teal, came dropping down. I shot two and then a third before it was black dark. My feet were freezing and my hands were blue with cold when I got off the marsh and took stock of myself. I was a little more damp than I had expected to be but not too wretched to be discouraged.

A week later I was back again and delighted to find that the teal were still as fond of the place as ever. This time I took a gorse branch with me and stuck it in the ground so that I could sit more or less in a normal position. The incoming teal shunned the place at first. As it grew darker they ignored the new feature of the marsh. I managed a brace and left before it was quite dark. The following week my gorse bush had been accepted as a landmark. The teal came to drop all round it without veering away or waiting until it was so dark that it made no difference. I didn't tell anyone about my secret marsh but perhaps most of my acquaintances would have fought shy of flighting with their legs in freezing water and more than once discovering that a ring of ice had 'grown' on the waders at the waterline!

Flighting on this grim little marsh went on for weeks. The teal that gathered there were occasionally joined by one or two mallard and there were snipe, but in the main it was a place of teal and I never discovered what it was that made it so. That they were estuary birds gathered as a result of migration seemed most likely. Teal on estuaries and rivers flight in company to rival homing pigeons in the way they sweep along, rising and falling, twisting and turning, but the way they came in to this marsh suggested that first one or two left the tidal water and came inland and the whole flock followed with a rush to dive headlong to the rushes, stand in the air with their wings spread and drop directly to cover. Once they were down their conversation was tantalizing. If I flushed them the drakes would protest as they rushed away. I found it hard to recover any that happened to fall in the round rushes, for they had the same ability to conceal themselves as the mallard in the barley, and I would hold my fire if it seemed inevitable that a duck would tumble in a place where I might not be able to discover it again. Once among the drakes I took home I found one I thought to be an American bird and I suppose I should have had it checked by an expert.

The estuary and riverside teal flight was never quite so exciting, or as reliable, as the flights I enjoyed on the marsh, but I always experienced an almost unnerving thrill to see teal on their way upriver. It was their speed that intrigued me and the timing of their manoeuvres as they made their concerted turns and climbs. Here they would come, travelling the course of the river half a mile or more below me at one minute and then, having swept overhead, speeding away on up a minute later. Who could display cool-headed marksmanship when things like this were happening? No one, I always felt, but the sort of man who aimed not at duck but at targets. The flight would be perhaps thirty yards above me and I would watch a solitary duck breaking out of the pattern and coming roll-ing down while the remainder rushed on, radiating slightly and drawing together in due time to go on right out of sight, and perhaps in a quarter of an hour a second flight would come, seeming to be even faster than the first, and I would watch them as they cut a corner of the water and eluded me away on the far side, or perhaps they would turn and take me unawares, slipping behind me when I was balanced to shoot in front.

Occasionally the river robbed me, for my solitary teal would fall out in the water and I could neither intercept it nor come up with it where it came aground. Sometimes the reeds, as tall as my shoulder, made an impenetrable screen beyond or in the midst of which my tasty little duck lay. On the river I often made excuses for myself. Teal, after all, are masters of the air. No other duck can do what a teal can do, and they are not a big target. I admit that I shot them mainly because I enjoyed eating them. I have eaten all sorts of fish and fowl. I rate the teal as the best eating of all, better even than the delicate flesh of a nice sea trout. It was, indeed, often much easier to get a fish from the river than make a bag of teal and one teal leaves the average man with an appetite for a second. The old hands, discovering a pond or a waterhole that teal loved to come to, would feed the place with grain, for teal, though they are primarily plankton and weed-feeders, are not averse to being corn fed. The feeding business never appealed to me very much and this was not because teal seemed to desert a pond completely after they had been baited and shot. I just had a soft spot for teal, as I always had for partridges though I never refused either for my supper!

A right and left at teal is inclined to inflate the ego a little, especially if one has read the exploits of famous shots and accepted their valuation of the sporting qualities of different sorts of game and fowl. It satisfied me when on odd occasions I brought down a brace of teal. They always seemed to fly fast which isn't the case with woodcock. Once when I had been singularly unsuccessful in my efforts to intercept teal coming up the river at dusk I managed, at the very last moment, to shoot a right and left and picked both birds from the short grass of the field behind me. As I was making my way on to the road to walk home I met an old man who had been leaning on the drystone wall, listening to my shooting down below.

'Them wee teals is fast,' he said, 'hellish fast. It takes a good shot to put them down when they're climbin' the way they climb.'

I agreed. The brace of teal were in my hand. I had brought no bag and the old fellow could count. He had counted my twelve or fourteen attempts to shoot teal and the white feathers of my victims enabled him to tell just how many I had in my hand.

'I managed two with my last two shots,' I said. 'You don't get a left and right every day.'

'No sir,' he agreed. 'That would be so, I imagine. A right and left. That's one down with the right barrel and one with the left?'

I said that it was.

'Just so, just so,' he remarked.

I had walked perhaps ten yards when he called after me. 'Would it be so even if you missed ten or eleven in between?'

There is a certain kind of old countryman who believes nothing he hasn't seen with his own two eyes.

Wigeon Ways

THE wigeon is a salt-water duck. It is found inland, of course, but its proper place is on the open water, the muddy rivermouth, the plain of the sea. Its proper food is the sea grass, though it feeds on a variety of other things as well. There are people who let the little teal go because it is small, downy and not very much to look at on a dish. The wigeon is a fowl with more to pick at, and, if the fowler forgets his stomach long enough to weigh other attributes of the sea duck, it is often almost as fast in flight as the erratic teal and certainly taxes his marksmanship a great deal more than the mallard. Stand and watch duck being flushed from a marsh. The teal go razoring away. The wigeon have a certain turn of speed. The mallard lumber into the air by comparison with them, and look as big as Canada geese when both are passing overhead. The whew duck, as the wigeon are sometimes called, whistle when they are coming in to feed on the marsh. They are in, and away again, a great deal faster than the mallard that suddenly detect the fowler's presence behind the old thorn tree. There is more excitement in the departure of startled wigeon than in the slow, once-and-for-all ascent of the mallard deserting the marsh with a long, slow angle of flight and a steady circling as they gain height.

The wigeon is a different sort of duck. It doesn't really belong to the common haunts of teal and mallard. Its behaviour is the behaviour of a species of fowl that knows the greatest safety on the open sea. It roosts on the water, snoozing the afternoon away in company with a hundred more, or occasionally with great rafts of duck that rise and fall with the waves, looking like floating wreckage. When the sea grass is faintly moving the wigeon doesn't feed as a mallard often feeds, up-ending, but in a strange way resembles a domestic duck as it paddles in the shallows, dipping and scooping and swimming on. Sea grass or zostera is all that the wigeon asks. Where the sea grass grows the wigeon goes, and the fowler too, but the fowler must wait his time. The wigeon, unless it is rocked by an angry sea, will stay on the water, swinging like a moored craft, head resting on breast. The scene, you will discover if you carry glasses, is reminiscent of the gregarious roosting of birds on sandbanks, gulls on the grass field, jackdaws clustering in a large elm or ash tree. Time has no meaning. The birds are asleep or comatose until the moment comes when one resettles its flight feathers, a few drakes seem to cock their tails and become alert. The awakening is infectious. A wand had been waved. The pack is about to rise, and who can say what triggers this movement and changes the appearance of the long line of fowl stretching across the bay?

This, if you are lying in the sand dunes, is the moment for which you have kept your vigil. The wind carries the spray of salt and picks up the sand and whirls it into the conifer trees high up on the shore fields. The sand stings your hands and impairs your vision. The light begins to fail. Was it better than this a week ago? Were the wigeon farther out? Were there as many of them moored out there? The exact number will only be known when they begin to come, a black drove of duck sweeping across the sand, filling the streaks of dying day, blotting the sky for a minute or two, and whistling 'wheeo, wheeo'. There is hardly a time when they come exactly as the fowler would have them come—directly overhead—for there is no flight line that can be marked with landmarks, only the tide line, the flanks of the sleeping monster running wet, the way to the river and the sea grass that grows in the tidal water.

It may be that you could find wigeon inland, feeding in company with teal and mallard, drakes chasing each other and making their harsh cry now and again, but never in such numbers as on the seaboard, the shore, the estuary, never as exciting as they are when they come in from the open sea, low, skimming higher, going away like leaves in a high wind. On a clear day you can admire them as they rest on the water, knowing them by their cocked tails, the white brand on the flanks, the buff crest, the almost pink breast, the contrast of black and white. They are as handsome as the handsomest of mallard or teal, and they have something about them that only migrant fowl have. Where were they before they began to gather in the estuary in October? Where did they nest and how did they come? Where will they go when they take their leave in late February or March? This is a romantic fowler's dream. The wigeon belongs away beyond the horizon. It crosses the waste of seas. Like the pinkfeet, it breeds elsewhere, and flying away it goes out to endless horizons stretching into Northern Europe, to Asia, places the man on the estuary has never seen.

There is always something mysterious about the migrant fowl so far as I am concerned. I see inland seas and tall reeds, places where otters roll and frolic in the water and shallow boats are poled along by bearded fowlers with Slavonic or Mongolian faces. The wigeon whistles in the dark sky and it might be the sky of Russia or Turkistan and I would willingly exchange my modern gun for the long iron-barrelled fowling-piece of the peasant in the marsh I shall never see.

Once I spent a day waiting for wigeon to come off a creeping tide, lying in a foxhole dug in the peat of the seaboard marsh. I discovered them there by accident when I went down to walk the marsh after the geese had left the mud. They floated in a long wavering line far out where the tide seemed reluctant to turn. I went over the side of the sea wall to look at a net washed among the elephant-like lumps of eroded clay lying where the mud began, and with the ruined net in my hand I stood staring at the far-off waterline and the haze of hills miles beyond it across the bay. It seemed that the waterline was disturbed, ruffled by something that at first I thought to be a sort of shelf in the sand. But then something moved— perhaps one of the roosting wigeon spread its wings and settled again—and I knew they were fowl of some kind. They had to be wigeon. A marsh farmer came down to look at some cattle he had grazing on the saltings, and I hurried across the plain of salt-whitened pasture to speak to him. Wigeon, he said. Wigeon by the hundred. They had been there for a while and no one had as yet discovered that they came up across the sand, turned and headed for the river estuary three or four miles farther along the shore. I wondered what to do to get in the right position to intercept them. The farmer shook his head. 'If there's a mallard or two already on that little flash,' he said, 'they come right down over them.' I knew then. I would dig myself a foxhole on the edge of the flash and put three or four rubber decoys on the water. When the wigeon came off it was unlikely that they would drop in to the decoys but they might come low to look at them as they went over. I plodded off back to base for a spade and the decoys. There was plenty of time, the farmer had assured me. The wigeon rarely moved until dusk so long as the wind didn't blow hard. They always went to the east though the next estuary was a favourite feeding-place for wigeon too.

A man who is absorbed in his sport doesn't pay much attention to the clock. He studies the light and considers the weather. If he walks a mile it will be worth it in the end. If he has to walk five it must still be weighed against his delight, or put down to experience if the exercise fails. It took me an hour or so to get off the marsh and arm myself for the return. The tide, it seemed, had hardly gained a dozen yards on the far-out mud. The wigeon were still the same distance from the water's edge, the hills across the water still hazed. There was nothing in the scene to inspire a poet or lift the spirit. I was on the edge of the Tundra, the fringe of the half-light or the edge of eternal night. The sky was evenly grey and heavy. The peat I dug stood in black mounds around me. The flash reflected the colourless sky and the rubber decoys that rode motionless on the water, each one moored by a lead weight and a pink tape. They were garish monstrosities, these rubber ducks, a compromise for mallard or wigeon, luridly coloured with orange, yellow, a slash of bright blue, white or green. They floated because they were designed to float, having an air-cavity underneath. In a wind they would heel over like a sailing-boat and bob on their anchors, as unlike duck balancing on the water as anything that could be contrived. I had no wooden decoys. The rubber ducks were light. I had plenty of time to watch them. Once, while I was day-dreaming in the peat bed I had dug for myself, a curlew came and sailed in right over my head to stand and look at my rubber ducks for a minute before he took himself off again, and once a small flight of golden plovers swept round and

round, tempting me to shoot, but I had a feeling that a single shot, no matter how much time elapsed before the wigeon rose, would tell them where danger lay. I did nothing and the plovers sailed on across the salting. When I raised myself and took a careful look out across the hump of the edge of the marsh I could see the wigeon still. They were coming in with the tide, like something being washed up on the shore, or so it seemed from where I watched. Perhaps they only seemed bigger because I wanted to see them coming in on the tide. They looked bigger and blacker. There were hundreds. The farmer had been right enough. There would be more wigeon coming off than a dozen fowlers could manage, but I didn't care very much. I was concerned that as the tide began to run a wind was getting up. The rubber ducks were rolling on their sides and behaving as decoys should never be allowed to behave. I got to my knees and crawled to the edge of the flash and went into the water as far as I dared to put the rubber monsters right. The wind quickly pushed them into the waterlogged bog cotton and the round rushes. I gave up trying to put them right. The wigeon might or might not take them for what they were supposed to be.

The tide was coming faster and the wind was whistling across the grass but I kept my head down and relied upon my ears to tell me that the wigeon were up. It seemed a long, long time before I heard the whistle, away to my right, a cock wigeon leading a stream of duck at top speed. I looked out of the corner of my eye. Wigeon were coming across the sea wall, the fences, the boulders, for three or four hundred yards. Hundreds and hundreds of wigeon, advancing on a broad front, sweeping off the sea and, I hoped, down across the decoys. I lay still. I could have counted the passing seconds by my heartbeats, by the pulse in my ears. All at once they were there, spread across above me, going faster than any duck I had ever aimed at, but obviously coming across the flash because there seemed to be duck on it. I struggled to rise. The whistling sound made me shake. They seemed to be whistling in my ear. I turned and looked into the wind, watching one particular bird as it came, growing larger and larger, heading directly for me. The moment was no more than a moment but somehow endless. I fired. The wigeon turned and came like a cannon ball right at me, crashing at my feet. Behind it the flight opened and spread. I took another bird as it climbed after the rest. It fell with a splash into the water. I loaded the gun and rose once again. The wigeon were higher, farther out, hurrying with the wind, hearing the whistling of neighbours, losing the sound of the gun because the wind whipped it away, but seeing me there beside that strip of water on the peat. I shot again and again. I had four duck to pick up when the fifth came low over the sea wall and I swung to it and put it down somewhere out of sight. Hundreds of wigeon had gone. There wasn't a single one still in sight. The tide was boiling into the mouth of the little creek close at hand. Deep water filled the holes around the great lumps of clay and rock. The muds had disappeared. Curlews were moving along the water's edge and I stood quite alone on the bleak and bare marsh reliving four or five minutes that were the substance of a day. The rubber decoys had to be gathered and returned to their rightful owner. I could hardly believe that they had really done what they were designed to do. The wigeon had come low, and they had come directly over the flash, but then they might have done so without the bizarre rubber ducks crowding in the round rushes like small boats washed ashore.

What does a duck see, and how carefully does it study what it sees? I have always had a feeling that duck, like trout and most humans, look once and hardly ever look closely. Once the image has been registered as safe or dangerous some serious disturbance is necessary to dispel that image. Floating beer bottles might have served just as well on this occasion, although to bring the wigeon down it would certainly have taken a more presentable setting of decoys, and perhaps decoys plainly showing the white flank of the species, if not the cocked tail and the poll-markings.

I confess to a crime which I committed on another occasion when in almost identical circumstances I waited for wigeon to come off the sea. Once again there were rubber decoys on a flash and I had company in the shape of three or four companions who had all made foxholes for themselves around a piece of water across which the incoming wigeon were expected to flight. The tide was rougher that day and the sky was bright and clear. The sun was high when the wigeon began to show signs of moving, taking short leap-frogging flights, one pack across another, and exciting the watchers around the flash.

A lookout was kept by one of the party who was better situated than the rest. When he announced that the whole mass of wigeon were up we stared at the grass and the moss before our faces until we were cross-eyed and stayed that way, so that no premature glint of an upturned countenance would make the wigeon turn. I was hugging to my breast an automatic shotgun loaded with five cart-ridges. I hoped to fire two, or perhaps three shots, and give a good account of myself among fowlers who were marks-men. All at once the sound of wings overhead brought me to my knees, and kneeling, I began to shoot at the duck against the sun, one, two, three, four duck hung in the air and fell before the echo of the fifth shot had sounded. I had all but achieved the feat of five birds with five shots. My companions sprang to their feet and cheered. They had never seen such marksmanship. I didn't cheer. I didn't bow. I looked at the duck that lay on the field.

Four handsome shelduck—protected birds! There was nothing I could say. Why were they not wigeon? Wigeon had risen from the sea and wigeon were still sweeping away across the mud, half a mile or more away. One solitary shelduck, the only survivor of the flight of five that had come between me and the sun, flew on. I stood dejectedly watching that shelduck as it departed and then went and picked up the evidence of my crime and took and buried it in a creek, pulling the bank down to cover the corpses. The tide came and washed them out again and my overburdening guilt made me go back and repeat the interment.

The gun I used was that famous make of automatic known as a Browning. At Christmas time I received a card addressed to Mr Browning. Browning was carefully crossed out and replaced by Shelley, a joke which still disturbs my peace of mind, even when I recall that the duck were black against the sun, for a shelduck is a great deal bigger than a wigeon, and by no stretch of imagination can their flight be mistaken one for the other! It was a lesson which I suppose in one way or another many fowlers need, or have had. I knew the wigeon and its ways before I ever saw a shelduck, for shelduck aren't common everywhere. Confusion is hard to justify and those who are law-abiding will say without hesitation that no one should shoot at any bird he cannot identify when he pulls the trigger. The wigeon were whistling. They had risen. They wheeled, I discovered, two hundred yards away and passed between our position and the sun. In the meantime, a lumbering flight of shelduck had come across the marsh and looked down at the gaudy rubber ducks that floated on the water, betraying me and making me do something that has inhibited me ever since. They were very handsome birds. Now and again someone asks me if I ever tasted a shelduck. I never have. I trust I may never put up a gun at one again, let alone shoot one.

12

Lesser Fowl

W HAT I have chosen to call the lesser fowl are, in general, all the smaller birds of the marsh and estuary that live on or about the water, a variety of small fowl that may legitimately be called the fowler's bag. There are, of course, a great number of gregarious shore and marsh birds, and some more solitary species, which are protected, and the man who goes in pursuit of the lesser fowl on the shore must avoid the mistakes that may lead to his being prosecuted for wantonly killing fowl that should not be shot. There are excellent booklets which enable the fowler to understand the difference between a redshank and a greenshank, if the name is not enough, and to know the godwits. With the larger fowl it may be that the fowler learns to identify the pinkfeet or the greylag because the particular species is the commonest sort on the shore where he lives. A black goose will give him occasion to pause and wonder if it isn't smaller or differently marked from the Canada goose, which is the only sort of black goose to which he may raise his gun. On the shore the fowler may wait a long time for geese and the wigeon may stay far out on the water and flight where he cannot reach them. In the meantime, the banks and depressions remain populated by smaller fowl of all kinds. Although he may study books and pamphlets, recognition, to a standard that will enable him to shoot when the opportunity presents itself, depends on observation and familiarity with the habits of all the smaller fowl of the marsh and shore.

It is a sad fact that the worst crimes of the gun-happy, would-be fowlers are committed on marsh and estuary when legitimate quarry is scarce. There are many people who hardly know a wigeon from a merganser or a mute swan from a greylag, whether they be in the air or at roost. With the smaller species the identification of fowl is complicated because some of them are not only gregarious but intermingle with flocks of different kinds of fowl. Some are hard to identify against the kind of light a fowler may encounter when he goes abroad in the early day, or just before nightfall. The smaller birds of the marsh and drains and creeks sit in company between feeding times. Grey plovers are so unlike the green plover and, for that matter, the golden plover that there is no danger of confusion. The fowler knows that once green plovers were shot in his part of the world but now they are protected. He must shoot a fair bag of little golden plovers to make a meal but he has more chance of a dish of golden plovers than a dish of snipe. The snipe is much harder to bring down than any plover.

There are two sorts of snipe that come within the category of fowler's birds, the little jack and the common snipe. A great snipe is listed, but great snipe are mainly out-of-season visitors and need hardly be considered. There are also the curlews, the whimbrel, a lesser breed of the curlew family and the every-day curlew of moor and marsh and estuary, the redshank and the bar-tailed godwit. Here and there on the marsh and in the sheltered corners of seaboard thickets a woodcock will rise and flicker away like a nervous bat, but the woodcock is a game bird even though, like the marsh pheasant, it not infrequently finds itself in the fowler's bag. These are the fowler's quarry. He must be able to identify them and know what the protected species are, ringed and stone plovers, dunlins, knots, stints and a dozen more. He must let them pass, hold his fire whenever he is in doubt, as he would when the coloured duck fly, or divers, grebes and other sorts of seafowl tempt him.

The grey plover hurries across the rough pasture of the marshes, sinking down to land in the coarse sedges where the marsh cattle graze, or comes unpredictably along the shoreline to rise on the ridge of pebbles and turn and rush away at the sight of the man wandering the high water mark with a gun under his arm and the labrador at his heel. I have eaten many dozens of golden plover but never a grey. I can't say when I always gave my bag away. I have a sentimental regard for the grey plover. It has what I call a china ornament look when it is on a field or along the shore.

I was never inhibited by the behaviour of the little golden plover, however, because the golden plover had a tantalizing habit of coming over our fields when I was a boy, rather like a flight of starlings, down on this meadow for ten minutes or so, up and away in a circle and down into the next field. On a wet, hazy day I would come through a gateway and up would go the golden plovers, over my head they would fly, swinging down again not thirty yards from me. Get some plovers, my elders would suggest. There is nothing nicer than a dish of little golden plover, and out I would go to shoot them while they were there on the green pasture. Sometimes I would make a bag in a very short time. I often brought down more birds than I expected, but I never seriously persecuted them for they had a butterfly way of being there one day and absent the next.

Snipe are something quite different. They may be in a marsh or a creek in considerable numbers but their flight is a solo flight. They make an individual bid to escape the fowler. The little jack, which may be in the same stretch of marsh as the common snipe, loops and leapfrogs from place to place, making a short flight. It is about the most pathetic sight that anyone ever saw on his supper plate, like the small blue fist of a child. I have long since given up pursuit of the jack snipe, but the common snipe has tempted me all my life. I might have claimed to be a fair shot but for the hundreds of times I have bungled snipe shooting. The snipe rockets into the air, plasters itself against the rain-swept, cloudy sky, seems to run across the heavens like a spider on the ceiling, arcing away and appearing deceptively large when it is already far out of gunshot. Whether they rise from a heavily grown bog of grasses and rushes or the gutters of a marsh, snipe, I am sure, time their departure beyond the point of man's alertness and his judgement. Either they spring into the air before I am ready for them, or after I have reached the very peak of tension, walking forward and waiting for the thing to be triggered off. Once a flight of snipe begins I stand in awe, seeing the first one or two giving warning to more and the whole company of feeding snipe leaving with a sporadic series of bursts that a man who contrives a fireworks display might envy. There seems to be a sort of invisible cord drawing one after another into the sky when the first bird goes slashing away, yet two or three more lie close and only rocket when a wave of calm has passed along the line of guns walking the marsh.

This is snipe shooting so far as I am concerned. I have never been able to record right and left. I have rarely had a day that would equal one enjoyed by men who either are born with wonderful co-ordination of hand and eye, or have trained themselves exclusively in the art of snipe shooting. Once, I recall, it did happen to me. I went into a flooded marsh in the bright sunshine of a freakish November morning. The snipe were there and my eye was in, as they say. Snipe are almost unpredictable because they have a marvellous ability to sense a change in weather. No one can guarantee that they will be plentiful on a marsh that hasn't been carefully watched, but on this occasion everything was right. The snipe were more plentiful than I needed them to be. They rose at regular intervals. The wind, such as it was, was in my face, and carried the sound of my approach away from the roosting birds. As I came within shooting distance individual snipe presented themselves. I had time to breathe, and time to calm my nerves, perhaps. I didn't miss one. I walked on feeling that at last it had come to me. I could shoot snipe with the best of them. Perhaps it had something to do with the atmosphere and humidity. I have often thought that a moist atmosphere, which must surely affect the feathers of all fast-flying birds, slows flight. Duck, teal in particular, always seem to climb and dive faster on a cold dry day than on an overcast or wet day. Woodcock certainly lumber through the glades of the wood when the leaves and branches are dripping with moisture but they are no slow-coaches when everything is frozen hard.

The fowler who spends his time looking for lesser fowl between duck flights or flights of geese doesn't make great bags of snipe, unless he has spent a lot of time and money acquiring skill. He potters the shoreline, walks up the creeks, peers over the sea wall and waits, perhaps for a curlew flight. Curlew have a habit of flying off the shoreland fields late in the day in cold weather. Like all other sorts of fowl, they are sensitive to falling temperature since a hardening of the ground, a heavy frost, means greater difficulty in boring for food. The estuary, because of the salt, is always much slower to stiffen and freeze. The curlew will roost on the grass fields and the pastures inland or sail about in the darkness from one place to the other, but there are conditions in which large numbers will head for the open sands, the far-out mounds and the depressions that lead to the hidden water channels in which, with many other estuary-feeding birds, they love to rest.

I remember waiting on the Solway shore for a flight of curlews a farmer had noticed each evening when he was moving cattle from the saltings. The inland fields were full of curlews. I had driven along narrow roads and seen hundreds of them. They came over the bank and down across the sand each evening, going as fast as anything he had ever seen, skidding through the air, the farmer said; a wing turned and the long beak outstretched and the bird was away, hundreds of yards out in less time than it took to blink. I sat in below a mound of eroding clay and boulders. The curlews were a long time coming. It seemed to me that the wind was trying to turn the stunted trees over and make them grow in the opposite direction. Little bits of grass and dead leaves from far back across the fields came rushing at me when I put my head up to look for the curlews. The sky lowered. Night was almost upon me when they began to come. I brushed wind tears from my eyes and began to shoot. The first bird I brought down fell far out in the open sand. I didn't walk to recover it until it was all over, for I shot curlews when I could sight them, and most of them were so fast that I could hardly believe that they hadn't been figments of my imagination. I saw them and I didn't see them. They went into the brown distance and they were gone. One fell in a pool and I paced the distance. It was three hundred yards from where I had been standing. But others fell farther out. The nearest was a hundred yards away. I gave up shooting and watched them coming and vanishing against the darkening background of the bare, bleak sands. Once in a while I heard them call. The wind whipped the sound away just as it propelled the birds over my head. I picked up my empty cartridge cases to keep the place from being advertised, but I didn't go back. I had had a curlew flight to end all curlew flights. There were two whimbrels among the birds I picked up.

Bar-tailed godwits and redshanks I have left alone, perhaps because I haven't hunted the shore in the manner of some more predatory fowlers. In the marsh I have hunted the marsh pheasant and the woodcock, and, I hasten to add, I have been sure that I had the necessary game licence to do so—a game licence isn't needed for every-day fowl, of course. The woodcock and the marsh pheasant have a way of sitting tight that is disconcerting to the fowler when at last he does flush them. It may be that he is hoping to put up a brace of teal from a drain or a pool, and crossing the rushes he puts the pheasant to flight. If he does, an extraordinary number of times he will discover that the marsh pheasant is a cunning bird. It is much more a bird of the ground than the pheasant flushed from game covers. It jouks in the open and leaves droppings in a place it has used several times. It calls as it goes to roost in the clump of round rushes or the patch of old dead grass. When it moves as the fowler comes through, it angles its way from cover to cover, hurrying up a depression, going smoothly across an open patch so that it hardly catches the eye of the most keen observer looking far ahead and well beyond the ranging dog. This pheasant is a descendant of the old stock from the East, a bird that properly belongs in the swamps and among the reeds and rushes and twisted trees. The fowler who outwits the marsh cock puts in his bag a crafty bird indeed, and generally an old one with long spurs.

The woodcock has a different background. In the main

he is a visitor, a winter migrant. He may prefer the hazel thickets and the hollows of more civilized country than the marshes, but in hard times he will be near the soft terrain where the flooding drains keep the ground in a boggy state and the food of the boring birds nearer the surface. I have dined on woodcock every year for more years than I can remember. A time was when I would put the little wing-tip feather in my hatband as a sort of advertisement of my shooting prowess, but to be truthful woodcock are only difficult targets on cold days and among close-growing trees and bushes, through which they almost tumble in an odd, top-heavy flight. On a dull day a woodcock is no more adept in the air than an old hen. He may never be compared to the snipe, the teal or the wigeon under any circumstances. It is only hard to get a right and left at woodcock because they rarely rise from a clearing to oblige. When they do, their exits are close at hand. It does, indeed, take some resourcefulness and presence of mind to cope with woodcock that spring into the air in confined places. Not many fowlers are tested by woodcock—and not many have witnesses if they happen to shoot a brace!

Some years ago I was waiting on the edge of a fir plantation leading to a large expanse of water from which we hoped to have a flight of mallard and wigeon. The wigeon were in from the sea, for the cold weather had set in. Mallard flighted regularly to their feeding-places on near-by marshes, but the flighting opportunity in that place was both restricted and brief. When duck came off they circled the water and flew overhead barely within range and in a minute or two it was all over. I had two companions sharing my stand at the head of a ride leading down to the water. Immediately in front of us, between the forest fence and the firs, was a planting of smaller conifers. The situation gave the duck some chance of spotting us before they came overhead, but had we stood closer to the trees we wouldn't have had an opportunity to shoot until the duck were over and beyond us. As it came near the time for the flight we could hear drakes quarrelling out on the lake, and that excited conversation that heralds the take-off, and then all at once a pause told us that the duck were airborne. At that moment we tried not to look at the sky but out of the corner of my eye, as the duck came, I saw a woodcock flickering across the tops of the high trees. I shot and it came down. I swung on a duck immediately overhead and missed, and then a second woodcock rushed over the small trees and I shot and brought it down. I was using a five-shot gun.

There it was. I had made a mess of my opportunity to bring down a mallard or a wigeon, but I had shot a right and left at woodcock! Both birds had been falling through the air at the same time, technically a right and left, if the miss in between could be discounted. What was more, I had witnesses. There is a well-known club that admits to membership those who have shot a woodcock right and left in the presence of two witnesses. In addition to membership of the club the marksman is sent a bottle of fine liqueur. I scratched my head and wondered how I stood. Could I honestly claim that I had achieved the feat? I sat down the following day and wrote about my experience. I didn't qualify for membership of the club. I should have said nothing about that quick snap shot at the high duck. My witnesses weren't aware that I had even tried to shoot a duck, and had mumbled something about allowing myself to be distracted by woodcock. The makers of the brandy had sympathy. They wrote me a letter, said they hoped that I would keep on trying. As solace they sent me half a bottle of their excellent product and I drank their health. I may be lucky one day, but I feel that it requires more than luck to have two witnesses at one's elbow when such an opportunity presents itself.

13

The Wild Goose

THE very sight or sound of the wild goose fills me with a nostalgia for yesterday, and a time when the migrating geese belonged to the autumn along with shorn stubbles, mist in the hollows, black earth thrown across an untidy potato field as the digger went on its way. For everyone who becomes a fowler the geese have a particular magic.

Mine was spun long ago when I helped the potato diggers one autumn day. I was barely knee-high, but there I was doing my best to retrieve potatoes from the earth and carrying half-cans, or perhaps only one or two, to the place where they were being loaded. A covey of partridges had gone out of the weeds along the potato rows where the heavy-footed Clydesdale horses were pulling the machine and I stopped to watch them fly. They rose over the hump of the hill and all planed together in a glide over the boundary hedge. That was the last I saw of them, but as I stared in the direction in which they had gone I saw the long wavering line of birds high in the sky, so high that they were close to the roof of the world, it seemed. Behind the first line came a second, and far away a third, and then a fourth flight, as small as flies above the hedge on a summer's evening. I stood and stared and forgot the partridges and the potatoes.

The geese came steadily on, wheeling in the heavens and changing course over the bay, beating on to the estuaries and the mudbanks to the east and south. They called to one another as they travelled, making a joyful babble of sound that came faintly down, emphasizing how remote they were from the land and the people stooping and straightening to put potatoes in cans. I pointed to them and called to the women who were working along the row. They looked up, shaded their faces with their earth-crusted hands and nodded.

'The wild geese have come,' they said.

It was something that peasants in the field had said year after year since the beginning of cultivation. The geese had come again. If a year ever arrived when the geese didn't come surely it would be the end of the world? I stood and watched and no one asked me to carry any more potatoes, perhaps because I wasn't contributing very much to the harvest, but probably because some of them remembered a day when they, too, had marked the coming of the geese. It was autumn indeed, autumn when a new growth of mushrooms dotted the pasture, when the stubbles turned red and then bleached, when horses began to plough, the last lingering summer birds departed—and the geese came.

Where did they come from? Places like Iceland, said the old men, places away up in the north where they nested along the sides of lochs and out in the moss, places where the midges swarmed and there were few people, just lonely bays, hillocks and cliffs, covered with all kinds of fowl. I can't remember reading a book about the wild

geese when I was a boy, but all this I knew as a sailor's
son learns of foreign places, from the old men. In the
spring the light brightened every day and the geese went
back. Their return was never marked, any more than we
noticed the shading of the fields from fawn to pale green,
or other things that marked the season until suddenly the
geese were gone, the willows were budding, the plovers
flying over the ploughed field.

In autumn, when the great migration took place, even
the sky had a special colour, a sort of pastel shade of silver
and grey and an immobility, a high dome, in which the
winter geese came southwards. Sometimes their passing
was heralded by farm geese whose hearing was more
acute than ours. After the farm geese had babbled away
for ten minutes or so we would see the reason for their
excitement: echelons of geese, so far up that they could
hardly be made out at first. In the quiet, still autumn
world with no tractors, no mechanical monsters propelled
by the internal combustion engine, the call of the farm
geese was heard away aloft. The wild geese talked back.
I used to watch this thing and have pity for the lumbering
domestic geese when they hurried across the grass and
flapped their wings. They would have gone with the wild
geese, it seemed; they would have flapped their way into
the cold wintry sky and hurried to join their wild relatives.
I was inclined to cry about that but after a while I saw
more of the wild goose, the goose on the stubble field,
the goose cropping the winter keep that the sheep needed,
the goose plundering the potato field and taking a toll of
everything the seaboard farmers left growing in their little
fields.

The goose is the biggest sort of fowl that a man with a
gun can bag. Swans are royal birds. A goose belongs to
the men who stalk it on the marsh, waylay it on its flight
from mud to stubbles or pasture, creep up on it when it
is promenading some inland field, or catch it taking a sail

on the fresh water of the loch. The expression 'wild goose chase' is a fair indication of the average man's success in pursuit of the greater fowl. A wild goose chase may occupy the uninitiated for not just a single day, but whole weeks of his life. There was a time when most fowl were comparatively unafraid of man. There are places still where this naïve behaviour can be witnessed yet, but the goose has always been a wary sort of fowl. Geese have proved themselves as good guardians of the citizen as any watch dog or yelping hound. The man who stalks a goose discovers the odd way in which the flock is automatically protected. While a hundred geese feed there is never a moment when two or three are not looking up and looking around, though they are never the same geese, or only very rarely the wary older birds.

The pattern is fascinating when one realizes that it must be the product of generations during which flocks of birds that greedily fed continually with their heads down were depleted. Geese were taught to be wary, conditioned to keep this kind of watch. Once the bird that has its head up discovers something that seems suspicious it remains on the watch and the next bird that pops its head up notices the danger, or the fixed pose of its neighbour, and it too remains on guard. In a moment the alert is communicated to the flock. Let the disturbance continue or become only a little more pronounced and the geese will take off. They are a species of fowl with extraordinarily keen sight. The cause for alarm may be in the creek a few hundred yards off, or out on the sand a mile away. Let the stalking fowler do what he may, once he has been detected he will be watched, even though a good proportion of the flock may resume feeding. Let him try to stalk and he will find that the geese are ready to rise as they never were when he kept himself concealed and made his approach in the dead ground of the creek, or the hollow in the sandhills.

Geese rise and fly with a leisurely wing beat, but like the curlew they cover more ground than they seem to, and in a moment or two they are a mile off, making an ellipse above the mud and carefully inspecting the territory upon which they plan to alight. Let the fowler rise and make his way into a depression in the marsh to resume the chase and maybe the tail-end of the flight will detect him or a solitary bird, a cripple that has been tagging on behind, will mark his progress. The game is a very old one and the geese are adept at anticipating the approach of the gunner. A creek crawler studies the wind, the tide, the lie of the land and the possible routes he may take to reach birds far out on the mud. Geese are a lure that has been the undoing of many an ardent fowler. There was hardly ever a more futile exercise devised by man than the casual pursuit of the wild goose in the open. At the time the geese rise the gunner will discover he is well out of range. By the time they pass him, to left or right, they will be high enough to escape his hail of shot. This is indeed a wild goose chase. Everyone who is untutored learns that it is something comparable to chasing butterflies in the soft breeze of a sunny summer's afternoon, or walking to the rainbow's end!

When you stalk the geese you may discover that they are already agitated to move on their own account. There is a ritual to the take-off that excites the fowler, whether he is within gunshot or not, a sort of parade on the open sands, first in one direction and then in another. It begins with one or two birds hurrying off, waddling as fast they can waddle with their heads held high and their wings flapping, but when they have gone a few yards and have encouraged only two or three more to join the parade they will about face and make a run in the opposite direction.

This will go on until the whole flock seems to be more concerned with rushing hither and thither than flying, and then, all at once, the excitement will die and with it the babbling that always accompanies such displays. After a period of wing-shuffling and settling the movement will begin again and go on until a small group will take the air and half-heartedly circle and return to the mud again. Perhaps the whole thing is a sort of competition for leadership and only when certain older birds decide that the time has come to take off do the geese take to the air in a body.

Whatever it is about, it makes the fowler's heart beat a little faster and his hackles rise, for there is something strangely primitive about the thing, an electric atmosphere that is fully charged when the flight takes place and all at once the air is filled with the sound of wings and the cry of the geese. I must admit that many times, with the ritual there to alert me, with the excitement increasing my pulse, I have failed to come out of the trance that the whole thing induces and the geese have risen and gone over me without my firing a single shot, this when I am no longer young or lacking in steadiness when I have a gun in my hands. The geese have a way of doing this to novices and beginners. Novices rise and shoot when they have no hope of bringing a goose down out of the sky or fumble when the moment comes to shoot. I am no longer a novice. It is more than nerves that stops me, a sort of amazement. There is no time to shoot when I stand and see the pinions of the goose waving, the tucked-up feet, the outstretched necks, the barred bellies, the soft grey and white feathers. Only when I remember this, and am prepared for my reaction, can I forestall myself, prompting my almost entranced brain with the message to shoot, shoot now!

There is a time when the geese are not quite so wary, of course, a brief period, when they have newly arrived; then they behave with much less caution. Green geese, the old fowlers call them, because they have come south for the first time, or have forgotten what happened in the previous winter. The young geese are slightly smaller, less strong on the wing than their elders. A toll may be taken of them when they first arrive to fly from mud to pasture. It was always like this. The fit survive. The unwary are eliminated.

In a matter of days the fowlers who know that a gift horse must never be looked in the face have taught the flight to watch the creeks, the hedges, the hollows along the marsh. In a week or two, unless the wind is strong and cloud hangs low, the geese will be climbing high to leave the mud, going away out beyond the tide to gain height and coming back again far up out of range. It takes far less than a season for the habit to be adopted. Depending on the disturbance and the intensity of the shooting, the geese will begin to know the danger spots in a week. The young birds become almost as wary as the flight leaders and the highly strung sentinels that wheel them away long before they reach the men standing in the gorse clumps or lining the hedges.

The lure of the wild goose gets into the blood of those who come to flight. It is something not unlike the lure of the great trout in the most remote loch, something quite beyond explanation or reason. The goose flies in over the marsh, four or five hundred feet beyond the tallest elm or ash, heading into the soft light of the setting sun. Anyone working on the pasture knows that this will happen afternoon after afternoon so long as the sky is clear and there is no wind, but the fowler comes and stands and watches as he clutches his useless fowling-piece. When the geese have gone steeply down to the far-out mud he will turn and make his pay out of the marsh again, persuading himself that in the morning things will be different. For once the flight will be at the expected time and not more than a gunshot up, and two or even three geese will fall. Tomorrow and then tomorrow, and at least a morning when the rain is turning to hail, when the clouds are low and the wind is strong. The geese come to left and right, finding their landmarks with difficulty, and one, flying wider than he should have done, breaks through the low cloud and is intercepted by a shot, turns in a slow, half circle, losing height. The fowler has his goose, if he can find it out there on the rain-beaten mud beyond the hurrying water of the creek. This is the fowler's morning, the day that he will talk about until he meets the old hand who can dig from his experience another day to put the whole thing to shame and into the shade, a day when the geese came in droves through the snow flurry, so near the waiting fowler that he could have touched them by waving his hat, one, two, three, six or maybe seven or eight geese, a double, a right and left with the eight bore. That was a morning to remember! The modest fowler has a practised ear. He knows when he is being put in his place by an old hand. He goes away and, instead of being content with what is his just reward, he dreams of doing what the old hand did—once in a lifetime.

The geese come and they go again. Here and there, however, one or two linger on the mud when the migration is past. This happens every year, it seems, because geese have a great loyalty to one another. A bird that is winged or suffers some slight injury which prevents it leaving for the breeding-grounds will be flanked by another, perhaps its mate, and they will remain, keeping one another company and picking up other left-behind birds scattered over the area. The fowlers watch these stay-behind fowl and consider their chances when the marsh fox is on her rounds to find food for her cubs. The fox is the scavenger of the marsh. When a wounded goose crashes far out in the wilderness the crows quarter the ground to eat its flesh before other scavengers arrive, but the fox is alert for the runner, the bird that flaps across the creek and painfully waddles out to the great plain of the mud. Once it finds the trail the cripple's fate is sealed. A bird that can still take to the air can sometimes recover and remains to feed on the shore fields and the marsh, gathering strength and renewing its stamina until it is fit to fly with the geese that come back in October. There are fowlers of a sort who pursue the injured bird to put it in the pot whether it deserves to be left in peace or not, a minority whose greed and callousness is without limit, but there always have been men of this sort and most of them are quickly identified and despised by self-respecting sportsmen. It is often the case that crippled birds are the result of the careless shooting of these very same individuals. The goose that survives the flight and summers on the mud deserves to be spared. I am never so sad as when I see the faltering, slow-flying bird that has been injured on some earlier occasion turning back out of the morning flight to go forlornly down to the mud, nor ever so angry as when I see some lumbering moron heading out to the wet sand in the hope of running it into the sand with the aid of a dog, or taking a second shot at extreme range to repeat the damage done a week before. The world is as it is, and not as we might like it to be!

14

Greylags and Pinkfeet

THERE was a rhyme my aunts used to chant to me when I was quite small. It was about the grey goose and the fox. We never saw a fox, for the countryside was much too well keepered for the fox to come out of the distant wilderness of the Galloway hills. Grey geese I knew. There were the geese of the farmyard, and the geese that flew overhead from time to time between October and February. The grey goose was the greylag, which came to the water-meadows in the mornings and flew back again to the mudflats and the shores of the estuary in the afternoon. All the geese that flew were 'greylag geese' so far as I was concerned. There may have been pinkfeet geese about, but I only knew them as the old people described them, the greylag geese of winter, and the greylag is properly designated a grey goose. It is named for its greyness. It has a fine grey head and is, so far as I am concerned, a more handsome bird than the brownish-

coloured pinkfeet goose. Greylags marked the day like
the creamery whistle and the distant train. People would
take out their watches and check the hour after they
heard the whistle, the train, and the geese. Ploughmen on
the high hill would look away across the moorland and
remark on the morning flight of greylags. It was time for
tea and scones to be brought to the field, the scones to be
unwrapped from newspaper and the hot tea poured into
a bowl while the ploughman crouched on his heels and
admired the geese steadily sailing in to the winds of the
river, babbling and circling and sinking lower and lower
until they touched down on the meadows with a last flash
of white underwing and an abrupt ending of their melodic
conversation.

In the afternoon, when the furrows had a cold look
about them and the horses' breath hung in steam about
their muzzles, the grey geese would suddenly begin to
talk again. Sometimes they were only audible when they
were climbing high above one of the white-washed, riverside farmsteads, or when the flight was silhouetted by the
pale winter sun shining on the bleached wilderness of the
moor, but the day was drawing to evening when it happened. A man who heard that sound expected soon to hear
the 'dropping-time' whistle, telling him he could unhitch
his chains and plod homewards with his team. There were
no other geese but grey geese, and the grey geese were
greylags. In time, of course, I discovered that grey geese
was a collective name covering the pinkfeet goose, bean
goose, whitefronts and lesser whitefronts, just as black
geese was a name for all the geese that were almost
entirely black or pied, the brent, the barnacle, the Canada
goose.

The greylag remains my favourite goose for nostalgic
reasons. It has the call of the farmyard goose, while the
pinkfeet yelps like a stoned dog, I often think. Fowlers
who take the trouble to watch the geese discover that by

comparison with the greylag the pinkfeet might well be called a brown-grey goose. It is easy to confuse the two at a distance and many a tumbling pinkfeet has been discovered to be a greylag, immature plumage and other details adding to the confusion until all the marks of the greylag and pinkfeet could be checked when the bird was lifted from the sand. As with the wagtails, grey, yellow and pied, there are features of the plumage, feet and beaks of geese that suggest a pinkfeet goose might be better designated by some other characteristic than its feet. The feet and legs of the greylag may be pink. The greylag is a greyhead, the pinkfeet a dark-headed goose with bars on its back. The bean goose, a much less common species of grey goose that comes out of the north-east (the pinkfeet and greylag come from the north-west, Greenland and Iceland in the main), also has at least one feature that some greylags display—yellow feet—although there the similarity ends. A whitefront isn't white-fronted by having a white breast. The white 'front' is the area above the base of its bill. Bird-watchers have no difficulty in separating the different species. Fowlers who have travelled a little, or stalked fowl in places where different species of geese are not uncommon, generally know their geese well.

The greylag holds on to the south-west of Scotland where I spent my early years. But the pinkfeet, they say, has gradually taken over territory solely inhabited by the greylag at one time. Geese frequent different places because they are particularly suited to those places. When the processes of agriculture change, when habitat of a particular kind diminishes in area, geese that depend on that habitat cease to frequent the place in the same numbers. Pinkfeet geese have found the Solway entirely to their liking. The goose of the Solway estuary is the pinkfeet, with the greylag making up the numbers, but it wasn't until I had left my spiritual home in the north that I came to know the pinkfeet goose at all. As far as I can remember no one shot a pinkfeet goose when I was a boy.

I had a nostalgic longing to go back north and hear the winter geese as I had heard them long ago. When the time came for my sentimental journey it wasn't unnatural for me to peer upwards at the sky once I had crossed the border beyond Carlisle, listen, as I was driving, for the call of the grey geese. They were there, as I knew they would be, flighting back out of the flat hinterland, along the course of a river, down a long wide valley, geese by the hundred and coming lower and lower with that exciting babble of sound that characterizes a flight. I stopped the car to listen to them. These weren't my geese, I began to think, and yet how could they be different from the geese that would be flying in the same November sunlight over the countryside in which my father had been born, a hundred miles or so to the west in Galloway? They were geese and they were coming in. Every fowler knows what a moving sight the evening flight can be. It is a spectacle. It marks the evening sky and advertises itself far and wide. Nothing can hide it, or change the strange silence that falls on the countryside when it is all over, the babble diminished and at last silenced, the geese settled far away out of sight on the thin line of the horizon of sand and sky.

While it lasts the flight stops most people in their tracks, if only for a minute or two. Old men look up as though assured of eternal life. The woods and hollows are filled with the musical sound, a liquid quality that is in the call of geese when they are far up above the hazels, the thorns and the hedge trees. Afterwards a crow calls, the bullock lows and owls cry. Out on the sand only the waders trill. The oyster-catchers converse when the geese have done talking. In a strange way the air seems colder, the fields less hospitable, the night's imminence more depressing and foreboding. This experience will be yours if you follow the steps to the marsh taken by most men who become interested in fowling. In time you will make a journey to some fowler's Mecca and talk about flight lines and grey geese, the prospect for the morning, the height at which geese fly when the air is calm and mist begins to gather in the marshland and fields.

Flight lines are the routes taken by geese in their daily coming and going. They are talked about by old hands who will bid you welcome and give you anything but the flight line that will guarantee you a goose to take home. Ask the old hand anything but this. He will tell you, if you are naïve enough to ask, just how far to lead a goose when you swing your gun, but he will make no appointment to take you with him tomorrow if he has 'kept' a flight line for two or three days. This is a fowler's secret, something like the cultivation of a plant, because yesterday he waited for the flight in a certain place and today in another, but for perhaps a week he has noted that a small flight of geese went over a particular place where no one shot at them. The knowledge is hoarded until the old hand decides that the geese are less wary on that line and fly lower there than anywhere else. The time has then come to shoot it. The old fowler knows he will be successful. When he has shot in that place and come away with his fair reward the less observant fowlers will flock to the same corner. The geese will fly higher, wider and more warily. They will veer away from the place and the old fowler will watch each morning until he discovers another flight line with the same advantage. There is no substitute for experience and the fowler can only learn in one way, or trust to luck, forgetting sometimes that the high-flying geese see much more than he imagines, the movement in the gorse, the glint of a gun barrel. One shot at a far-out flight of babbling pinkfeet geese may result in the lead dropping to pock-mark the wet sand and do no more damage than that, but be sure the geese become accus-

tomed to noting the direction from which danger threatens. Who can tell what all that babble in the morning sunlight is about?

I went back to the Solway, stopping short of what should have been my destination, saw the geese flighting, a Sunday sunset. They weren't my greylags of long ago, but I knew them. What I didn't know was how the world had changed! In the morning, in charge of a suitable guide, I gathered my gear, gun, torch, a stuffed valise to sit on, cartridges and the rest, and followed my leader into the waterholes and the peat drains that marked the way to the blackness of the shore, stumbling along a fence that divided salting from mud. I saw the fence when dawn broke. It loomed in the swirling mist, draped with grass left on the rusty wire by spring tides. It hung drunkenly above minor cliffs of slimy clay and straddled little creeks with posts suspended in mid-air and held there by the wire, while down below the backwash of the tide left dead bushes, bleached branches, wicker-work that might have been lobster-pots or potato baskets. After a long interval the day began to creep across the mud. Black-backed gulls made raucous cry. I lay in the no-man's-land of mud and heard the pinkfeet stirring. They were perhaps four or five hundred yards away, but it was a long, long time before they took off. When they were in the air the sudden blasting of guns took me by surprise and disturbed me much more than it disturbed the geese, I think. Not one goose fell. They climbed high and swung far out over the wet mud and the banks of sand. They were far too far up to be reached.

I felt then that the world had changed and I had slept. If I put up geese now I was in competition with men who lived in Salford and Bermondsey and Kent, and none of them had stood on the stubble field when they were three years old staring up at the geese in the sky, feeling the stones and the soft earth on the soles of their feet. The

geese belonged to the man who could bring them down.
They were like those tin targets wound round and round
by the shooting gallery men at the fair but much harder
to hit because no one would give anyone else a chance.
The peace of the morning was still being disturbed when
the last of the straggling geese came off two hours later.
Long plumes of smoke rose in the air and wavered and
vanished after some extra-long, black-powder fowling-
piece had been discharged, but even the long guns of the
most eccentric fowlers made no impression on the departing geese. The evening flight was much the same. This
time the geese were greeted with salvoes from hedgesides
and mounds covered with high gorse. They flew away up
against the bright sky of the evening. The longest gun
with the heaviest charge of shot and powder made no
impression but the barrage might have made sound
effects for a film of the second front. It was a week before
I saw a goose brought down. I think it was probably a
bird that was less able to gain height, because of some
previous mishap, than the rest of the flight with which
it was attempting to keep pace. Even so, it had to be
shared by more than one gun. The time was when I
could have filled a room with greylag geese if I had
wanted to.

Nowhere in Britain remains remote. The most lonely
wastes of far northern estuaries are just as likely to be the
scenes of desperate and wild shooting as the accessible
marshes and estuaries in the southern parts of the country.
Where there are no regulations to control how geese may
be flighted, and wardens to see that the wild men behave,
holes are dug away out in the sand so that the geese may
be shot as they rise. The biggest gun, the largest shot,
some men believe, gives them a prize which entitles them
to call themselves fowlers. Much of the deplorable con-
duct one hears about comes as a result of publicity, articles
and eulogies of wildfowling in out-of-the-way and little-

known corners, embellished accounts from the mouths of
braggarts, and pure imagination. The old fowlers know
the truth of these matters and shake their heads. They are
powerless to prevent abuse or correct the wildfire rumours
that bring would-be goose shooters out of their hiding-
places. The pinkfeet goose, the greylag, the whitefront are
migrants from the north. They are met by a leap-frogging
company of brigands who blast the Southport sands one
season, the Solway the next, the Wash, Wester Ross, if
need be, and the western seaboard of Ireland. From all I
hear, most of these adventurers return at length dis-
illusioned after a season or two. Perhaps they put away
their bright new guns and take up ski-ing or golf, but
there are always others stepping into their shoes, and the
geese are always thicker in the air in some dream estuary,
farther and farther away. A wild goose chase is a wild
goose chase, however far a man travels, I fear.

There is one consolation about it all. I see no threat to
the pinkfeet nor yet to the greylag. Neither diminishes in
numbers. The farmers of Perthshire protest that the greylag shouldn't be protected because it is a grazing bird that
rivals the sheep and deprives their stock of winter keep.
If the greylag count is down, it surely is a question of
habitat changing rather than the pressure of shooting.
Protecting geese under one blanket regulation might
please the bird-watchers, but it could hardly be relied upon
to preserve the grey geese from the effects of agricultural
changes. It wouldn't protect them from the farmers who
would never stand by while their barley, oats, wheat,
potatoes and grass were cropped down and ruined. Geese
could be culled by professional shooters, of course. There
might be support for this proposition among those who
gleefully think of filling up forms for compensation based
on estimated losses from the depredations of geese, but all
of this is supposition. Responsible fowlers and responsible
conservationists will undoubtedly see to it that whatever

controls come in the future they are based on fact and
logic, and not on emotion and mere supposition.

The black goose that has recovered on the Solway, the
barnacle which swarms on the Caerlaverock shore, was
always hammered by the fowlers who encountered these
somewhat tame geese of the far north-east before the law
proscribed the shooting of barnacles. I wouldn't suggest
that there are grounds for an open season on barnacles but
even if I did so, and could substantiate my case with fact,
the trend of legislation is finality. In this particular
instance I am content that it should be. Laws are rarely
relaxed, however. If the greylag is proscribed there may
come a day when a procession of heavy-ended gentlemen,
who never saw a goose fly except on the television screen,
will march through the division lobby and the marshes
will never know the fowler again. The very thought makes
me run back into the potato fields of my boyhood to see
the greylags fly, for the sky was high and clear. Laws
were comparatively simple, and uncomplicated, a blessing
I never appreciated.

15

Ancient Art

W H E N man's existence was primarily concerned with the means of surviving, living through one day to be there on the next, the more intelligent savage armed himself with weapons the use of which he had diligently practised. The man who lived on was the one who added a degree of cunning and an understanding of the ways of his quarry to the means he employed in hunting.

I suppose the decoy must be older than the spear or the sword. Certainly decoying by emulation, by the imitation of sounds made by other animals, is an almost inbuilt thing in man. The bird that feeds on a field, or swims on a pond or a creek, represents safety to the bird that flies in search of food or its own kind. To lure birds it is good to bait the ground, but it is better still to have birds on the ground already playing the role of Judas, betraying their own kind. Tethered birds, tame birds, pinioned fowl and, of course, effigies—stuffed, carved, moulded decoys—all have the power of attraction. No one knew this better than the ancient hunter. In tropical countries a husk of a gourd would serve. In the wilds of the north, when spring came, the Eskimo would mould a duck or goose with mud or peat and sit the rough decoy in some open place to bring the passing fowl down. The North American Indian lured his duck with decoys fashioned from woven reeds.

It is an odd thing that more sophisticated individuals make more elaborate decoys, adding details that have become essential, not because the fowl being decoyed make a more careful inspection of things in more civilized surroundings but because the mind must be satisfied. A good decoy has a prayer with it or the man who sets it achieves little success. Let me warn you about this before you embark on the business. A decoy to one man may be a work of art and to another an overpainted toy. On the mud or floating in the creek with a suitable mooring cord, a champagne bottle or two may serve as lures for duck if the shiny glass can be clothed in something suitable. The bird coming in doesn't react to the absence of eyes, the lifted head, the blue and white markings on tail and wings, or even to size, but to something else that is indefinable, a superficial rightness of situation, a pattern scanned briefly and accepted. There is much more to successful decoying than this, but little of the success depends on a pedantic approach, on imitation of the duck in detail, or even on the grouping of the decoys, though some settings are occasionally more productive than others.

A long time ago I shot a mallard drake coming in to a field of corn stooks on a wet evening. To amuse myself, and not with any thought of decoying, I set the bird in the stubbles with a few twigs, wondering if I could make it look natural. My efforts were reasonably successful. I had often set up pigeons in this way, but on this occasion I had no reason to hope that duck would come to the dead

mallard. I left it on the field while I went down to a hollow
to investigate a hare I had seen loping through the rushes.
On my way back I was surprised to see two mallard swinging in round the bird I had set up. It may have been that
the duck had come to that corner of the stooked field every
evening but they dropped not six yards from the dead one
and immediately began to feed. This is invariably the
behaviour of decoyed birds. When they drop the fact that
the lure which brought them down is still there on the
ground has no interest for them at all. They either fail to
recognize it, or are quite oblivious to it. If the decoy came
in to feed, those which follow begin to feed at once. I
managed to stalk the two mallard and shot one.

I was fascinated at the thought of luring duck on the
waterholes of the bog, but somehow I never got round to
it. There were duck in plenty to be flushed when I took
the trouble to wade out there. I never made a decoy. Mine
wasn't a decoying countryside. Decoys are for estuaries or
ponds and the business of decoying is an ancient art.

In time, of course, I took to the decoy, the rubber ducks
on pink strings so beloved of the amateur who carries a
bagful as a standby when fowl are hard to come by. I set
them on ponds and little water splashes and watched the
duck come in. It is a sport for the man with self-control,
and a sense of responsibility, for there are occasions when
a setting of floating decoys is lethal and a professional
fowler might make his fortune. The situation having been
chosen with care, the decoys placed, and the fowler in
cover, it is a matter of time before the duck come in.
When they come they fly with that relaxed, unwary flight
that only decoyed birds display. At times they fly right
into the mouth of the gun, wings spread, feet dropped,
bodies almost vertical. The fowler can pick his shot and
kill right and left, or, if he has a whit of compassion, rise
and give them warning before they are hung in mid-air.
I was content with the rubber decoys until on occasions

they blew into groups, overturned in the wind, or dipped with the pull of the current. I thought to make something better. I set about carving a wooden duck from a pine log. The carving was rough and the decoy was not a great success. It listed and needed a counter-balance of lead which in turn raised the 'plimsoll line'—submerged the duck—until it looked about to founder. It was heavy and I was far from pleased with my work. In the end I chopped it up for firewood. Wooden decoys are bulky, in any case, and a man who uses them must have easy access to water, not far to carry his load, or he must live on the edge of a creek in a place where he can put out his birds and bring them in whenever the fancy takes him.

Years before, in the days when I knew some wild characters who would as happily poach a deer as walk a footpath, I had numbered among my acquaintances a keen fowler who had gone away to live in the haunts of wildfowl, a remote estuary where he could stalk geese and lure mallard, wigeon and teal with decoys. Encountering him again one day, I was dismayed to discover that the years had tamed him. He was engaged on business far removed from the river or the marsh. It was all over, he said, sadly. The fire had gone out. His old dog was dead. His guns, wrapped in oily rags, were put away. He had forgotten the call of the geese, the alarm note of the hurrying teal. If I ever wanted one he could let me have the use of a marshman's gun, a solid eight bore, and two dufflebags of decoys that still had mud on them. I felt sad. It is hard to see the friends of one's youth wilting, losing their enthusiasm for things that were once the very breath of life to them. We looked at the marsh gun and talked about cartridges. The decoys were tipped on to the cellar floor. They were an assortment of wooden ducks, mallard and wigeon; each one, though caked in mud, had its cord and anchoring weight wrapped neatly about its neck. I picked them up and handled them.

'There is nothing to touch the wooden decoy,' said their owner. 'They ride better. They look more natural. They won't blow over and they don't get crushed out of shape if you leave them in the bag from one year to another. They don't perish!'

I little knew it, but I was embarking on the decoy business with a vengeance to become not only a whittler of wood, but a dauber, going into the glass eye business, exchanging models with friends abroad, buying timber of a special kind, discovering the lore of decoying as it has been practised in New England since the early days of the settlements there. With a thousand other more profitable things to do, I was allowing myself to fall for the lure. It wouldn't do to borrow these battle-scarred, mud-caked wooden ducks from my friend who would probably never again put them out. I made plans for carving my own. Use white pine, advised an American friend. Balsa wood, said another, for balsa wood is light and easy to carry, floating as prettily as cork, but balsa wood is soft and doesn't stand up to knocks. I had visions of the wooden decoys being bundled in and out of the car and the bag being tossed in a corner. I had to have a durable wood that was as near balsa as I could get. A friend recommended obechie wood and I was hopeful. Obechie is durable. It is light and buoyant. It is easily carved. I hurried off to the timber merchant, but he shook his head. Obechie, yes, he had read the name somewhere. It was one of those 'foreign' woods. Wouldn't beech do? I knew it wouldn't. Sycamore, he said, is easily carved, but it floats like teak. Calling on the coffin-maker in the village in which I used to live I mentioned my problem. The little man smiled. Wait on, he said, and leave it to him. He had a traveller coming. Perhaps he would take an order for a baulk of obechie. A fortnight later the coffin-maker confirmed that the wood was on its way. In due course it arrived and I sat down to work out how many wooden ducks I could make. I had visions of a squadron of them, some looking left, some looking right, some sleeping, ducks and drakes, mallard and wigeon.

In America, where the greatest skill in decoy-making was practised in the eighteenth and nineteenth centuries, they are particular about the scale of decoys. A mallard decoy, for instance, will always be larger than life, at least half as large again. There is a school that builds its decoys more than twice natural size, I believe. The old hands discovered that the larger-than-life decoy is more effective. I looked at my timber and did some calculations and decided that I would be content with life-size mallards. I could carry more of them. I planned to make at least five, but I couldn't make five if I made them jumbo-sized. In a short time I had built myself a set of life-like wooden ducks, painted them in the traditional colours of the decoy, in flat paint. They were eyeless, however. I mentioned this to a friend, a collector of decoys who lived in America. Obviously, he said, I had gone over the line. I had passed from being a fowler carving decoys to pretentions to another art. I would end up painting the feathers on my decoys and comparing them, perhaps, to the work of a famous American named Wheeler, whose beautiful carved decoys lacked only the call of the particular sort of fowl they represented to make them perfect. Teddy-bear eyes, suggested a friend in Arabia. Advice was coming to me from the four corners of the earth, for I had correspondents everywhere. Advice came and then the eyes themselves. I was put in touch with a man who had bought the stock-in-trade of a taxidermist and had no particular use for duck eyes. I rashly bought up his stock and by the next post a batch of eyes reached me from America, and then another batch. Some Americans put blue eyes in their decoys, some bright yellow ones! Some decoys have black eyes, some amber eyes with black pupils. In a short time all of my decoys were roosting on my workbench regarding me with their bright, shiny, intelligent eyes. They looked very real. The set of wigeon decoys upon which I exhausted my remaining supply of obechie wood never looked quite so lifelike as the mallard, but they were good enough. I took them off to the marsh and set them up. They worked. They worked like a charm. Duck came swinging round and skimming in to them whenever I put them out. I set them in all the recommended settings, line astern and 'vee' formation, in clusters and ones and twos. I almost gave up shooting duck and took simply to decoying them as an alternative!

Make your decoys, if I may advise you, a shade larger than life. Out on the rough water of the creek or estuary, life-sized decoys look small. The larger decoy is spotted sooner and has more drawing power. I have become convinced of this. Forget the eyes. They are quite unimportant and probably useless. Put the splashes of white on the right place; a mallard decoy will attract wigeon and a wigeon decoy mallard. The shape isn't so very important. It seems a more lifelike setting when two drakes keep company with perhaps four ducks or more and the heads of the ducks are set right or left, but a sleeping duck shouldn't be moored in fast water, and the setting that lies a long time on the same pond ceases to be a lure at all, except to the odd duck that passes.

It is hardly necessary to lure duck to a stubble field but I have seen dry-land decoys carved for this purpose, one of them from an old mangle roller. I was given such a decoy and after trying it on a field where it brought a duck in—with the help of one or two others, I must admit— I sent this unusual lure off to America. It was taken into a collection there and prized because it had been made and used by the keeper on a famous estate. It was something more than a curio.

The sending of the mangle-roller decoy to America had a sequel. The collector who received it, along with one of my own models, sought to express his appreciation in a practical way and ordered a decoy to be sent to me from the Bahamas, avoiding American tax. This decoy, when it arrived, turned out to be an Italian model, not of a duck, but a peewit. The peewit is partly mechanized. It has hinged wings which can be raised and lowered by a cord. It seems that in Italy the peewit is lured as well as duck. Old decoying experts would often enhance their setting with a sort of sideline bird, a gull or even a crow, which would be placed on a bank or the grass verge not far from the place upon which the duck decoys were moored. This touch added to the naturalness of the setting, it was felt. I have never used the cocky peewit with its daintily curled crest of leather along with my obechie mallards or wigeon, but one day I may, if only to discover if there is anything in the old-fashioned embellishment.

The decoy is something that the apprentice fowler may toy with and in time he will discover the art for himself. In the beginning, it was a device of the man who was desperately hungry and subsequently an art cultivated by the professionals. The ramifications of the art are limit- less. Even the goose is decoyed, though not so often or in so many places as it once was. A stuffed greylag goose looks very like the real thing when it stands on the mud or in the stubbles, but one goose doesn't make a setting any more than one wooden mallard does so.

The stance of the individual decoy is important, how- ever. As with duck, there is an attitude that is an alarm posture. Geese feeding or resting are undoubtedly more effective than stuffed birds set up by a taxidermist to look at the sky and show off the fine line of neck and head. The man who takes goose decoys to the marsh needs a large sack, and he must be careful to choose a sheltered situation or only put out his decoys where he can reset them if the wind disturbs them. There is no moment more exciting for the decoyer of fowl than that when he discovers his decoys have worked, when the passing bird begins to turn, lose height and, at last, come in. It is breathtaking and, for me, sometimes paralysing. It has everything about it that I experience when I see a fish beginning to turn and take the fly, coming up out of the deep clear water. This, I say to myself, is the moment and there is nothing to equal it. I know what my ancestors knew, and I have the knowledge a man needs to survive, whether I ever practise the art or not. A fowler who hasn't decoyed duck has missed something he should not miss, a thing that happens without warning, as hypnotic for the beholder as it is for the fowl being lured and I count the times I have experienced it among the minutes I have really lived.

16

Odd Birds

I T is no more than fair that, having taken you across the marshes, encouraged you on the estuary and the lonely places, I should give some account of the company I have persuaded you to join, for fowlers in the main comprise an assortment of odd birds. Consider, first of all, the sort of man who will stand by himself, hour after hour, fishing, wrapped in his own thoughts, living in his private world.

It pleases anglers to talk of the fraternity of anglers. Indeed anglers for the most part are kindly, relatively harmless individuals, ready to share their sandwiches, offer advice on the sort of flies or bait a newcomer should use, or even to supply some missing part of his equipment, but they are, nevertheless, individualists and one should never expect too much of the man who paddles his own canoe. In the matter of taking fish the generous angler will keep some small secret to himself though he gives everything else away. There are two things in his world, himself and his quarry.

With fowlers it is much the same. They will share experience, give you their bag, for many of them have no use for the duck they have shot, but expect from them little in the way of warm companionship. Each one is a born hunter, living for that moment when he meets his quarry and tests himself against it. The fraternity of fowlers is rather like the fraternity of blind men, in my experience. Each one walks alone.

Perhaps the whole business of waiting and watching, and the fact that success generally comes to an individual rather than to a company or a group, a twosome or party of three, makes the individual fowler uncommunicative, ungarrulous, unforthcoming. Consider men you have met intent upon their own affairs and you may have some idea of the taciturn fowler you may suddenly encounter as you come lumbering down into the creek, far out from the shingle and the shore of the estuary. There is no cheery welcome, for every minute you spent crossing open ground may have made useless every minute the hidden man crouched in his chosen place. A welcome is more than you can expect, but supposing that you came upon him after a careful stalk and won your way to the creek with all the fieldcraft of a fox, what happens now? Are you pleased to see him there, and will you cheerfully salute one another? The entrenched man is at least taken by surprise, put out by your sudden emergence. Are you to stay or move on, for if you stay the chances of each one of you may be halved. The hand of friendship is withheld. You say nothing and climb out over the mudbank to make lonely tracks for another mile or more. It couldn't be otherwise. You don't know one another and the chances are that you never will unless, of course, you belong to some organization devoting itself to the problem of eliminating selfishness among fowlers, regulating their behaviour on the estuary or marsh, and protecting their interests.

There are all kinds of wildfowling clubs (for those who put their faith in organizations) and one of these you may join in order to win your way on to the shore or the marsh. Fowlers, who are probably the greatest individualists in the sporting world, are hastening to do just that at this moment. There is, it seems, no other future for the sport, but when I was a boy, more than half a lifetime ago, fowlers were an entirely independent breed. There were geese on the mudbanks, geese on the meadows, duck on the river and in every waterhole for a hundred miles around. Communications were of a sort that didn't favour the weekend fowler, the man from the city, the butcher, baker and candlestick-maker, coming out to shoot. The well-to-do shot fowl. They came for a week or a month, wearing knickerbocker suits and deerstalkers. They were flanked by curly-coated retrievers, water spaniels, and even gamekeepers who as jealously guarded the duck shooting as they did the pheasant coverts.

Brushes with the gentry, the privileged, were few and far between. It was possible to trespass on a preserve and to be had up for poaching a pheasant, but a duck was something different. The duck might be fed on a pond or lured with decoys, but it belonged wherever it had a mind to go, and the cleverest keeper born has never been able to make mallard or wigeon fly precisely where his master would have them fly. The wealthy landowner might slaughter hand-reared and hand-fed ducks flushed from his reed-fringed pool and shoot coming and going from alternate sides of brush blinds, but this, after all, had always been his way, everything to excess and in extravagance. The fowler proper, the man who needed the sovereign in his pocket, worked at the business in his own way, day in and day out, making a living if he could, getting enough for bread and cheese for his family at best, or perhaps enough to buy a dram and soften the aspect of the grim world he saw about him. He wore no Norfolk jacket. His gun was hardly something to be handed round and admired as a masterpiece of the gunsmith's art, but it brought down the goose. It achieved remarkable results considering that it wasn't inlaid with silver, bore no monogram, lacked the delicate finish of the finest walnut stocks and fore-ends tipped with horn.

You have seen the way a man who fishes for his living gathers his catch and steps out of his little boat? The old fowler would come off the mud carrying his birds in the same way, like a harvester, a man bringing fruit from his own tree with a consciousness of achievement, an awareness of the purpose of things. The duck blasted on the private loch might in the end lie beside the birds the professional carried, and one would be as dead as the other, but difference was the whole world between them. The man who made his living at the business was harvesting, while the landowner was gratifying a lust, proving over and over again something he needed to demonstrate only once or twice, that a gun held straight fires straight.

There was one of these old professionals who hung about the town when I was a child. Often my grandfather pulled in his pony and engaged him in conversation about this and that. He was a one-armed man, but it was known that he was a marksman of great ability. When the geese were there it was harvest time. He propped the town wall between tides and only went down to shoot when he could make a bag. A one-armed man with a heavy goose gun, one might think, would make a poor showing, but this little fellow knew no handicap. He had come to accept that one arm must serve for two, and he would march down to the mud, creep out as far as the quicksands would allow, lie down and wait for the geese to arrive, and hardly ever come empty handed away, for he would roll over on his back, clamp the heavy gun to his shoulder, making a bracket of hand and arm, squint along that great iron pipe of the barrel, and pull the trigger. He might lurch and sway as he ran to retrieve a goose, but he hardly ever fell, and the wounded goose, if he happened to wound and not kill, was pursued by a desperate, determined man, a fox of the marsh, a wolf.

'In a wee while now,' he would say, in answer to the old man's question about his daily visit to the bay, 'when the tide is a wee bit farther back. I was there this morning. I stopped two.'

He always told the truth. Would-be fowlers envied him and sought to ingratiate themselves with him. He liked a dram, but a dram, or even a glass, wouldn't persuade him to take a companion, any more than he would have taken an accomplice to help him slay a pheasant or two in a field when he made one of his forays against the keepers. Geese and duck could be sold quite openly and the one-armed fowler spent most of his time studying their habits and flight lines in order to bring them to the game-dealer's shop. Whatever he discovered, and no matter how successful he was, he had no information to give to anyone, nor were those who sought to emulate him able to gain anything by shadowing him, for he had a way of vanishing from the scene, disappearing from his favourite corner of the town square, showing up for a minute or two down on the meadow fields and then fading into his background, losing himself in a hollow, crossing a safe place before the tide came, returning long afterwards by some other devious route and carrying with him perhaps two or three fat mallard, wigeon, teal or a goose. The town gossips said that he could charm the birds or that he got them by casting spells. His envious and jealous acquaintances—for he had no friends—said that he found geese shot by other people, that he retrieved them from the water and made a show of bringing them back but didn't sell half as many to the dealer as he made out, yet the dealer knew and we knew. If ever I wanted to be apprenticed to any man it was to the one-armed fowler I would have gone. He was, like some of the master poachers I met later, a craftsman.

Since you cannot meet the one-armed man, for he has lain in his grave now longer than my grandfather has done, though his brown-coated ghost carrying that long heavy gun may still go out across the sand, you may meet, even yet, an odd professional here and there. Geese are no longer offered for sale. It is illegal to sell a goose. The market for fowl in any quantity has retreated from the areas in which fowl are shot to places like London where dealers still issue price lists to professionals prepared to supply them with snipe, coots, waterhens, curlews, all the lesser waders as well as the ducks. The professional has never had much time for the sportsman and unless he combines his trade with acting as a guide to the would-be fowler visiting new ground you may expect little change from him. The professional guide is as God made him, an honest rogue, perhaps, an optimist with the stand-by remark upon his lips that 'you should have been here last Thursday'. He, and the solitary fowlers you encounter, will still keep secrets. He lives on his reputation for being able to get a goose when he wants one, though sometimes he marches back from the estuary with no more showing from his bag than a pair of rather battered goose wings belonging to a bird he brought down a year ago!

Some fall among thieves in this business of being guided. Some get drunk on tall tales, for the unscrupulous guide knows how fowlers live on dreams of geese flying low, wigeon blotting out the moon, mallard coming in to a creek though the mud is untidy with birds already brought down. Not every guide is a villain. There are some who are troubled by the fact that geese and duck can't be made to fly by order and apologize for the lack of frost, the soft weather, the calm twilights and the reluctance of the geese to come back from other and more favourable places. I have been guided by a man who daily sank into deeper despair at the lack of success I was encountering, though he knew well enough that I had seen many flights and many different winters. Remember that no one has all the answers. The guide may know the marsh but no one can predict the behaviour of fowl that have more than a premonition of change in the weather.

As for the rest of the odd birds, and they are migrant as well as local, they belong to all classes, all trades. They garb themselves in a variety of clothing, from wind-cheaters, anoraks and duffle coats to zippered oilskins and an assortment of headgear that a revolutionary army might wear, peaked caps, hoods, woolly hats and old-fashioned sou'westers. They are red-faced and plump, lean and hungry, tough for the most part, and scornful of overdone comfort. The majority of them wear thigh boots suitable for the marsh, that is boots that are not too tight on the leg, for a tight boot may be a man's undoing when he finds himself deep in the mire and might otherwise escape by slipping his leg out of the boot.

They dress according to their experience, you will find, this one remembering how his energies were exhausted when he was too well covered and that one having a fearful recollection of the pangs of exposure when his body began to lose its vital warmth. Talk with them, if you come up with them in the inn, and you will find that the convivial atmosphere transforms them, as though they had stepped upon a stage. Now, in the glow of the fire, they will talk about the marsh and the tide and the evening flight, the sound of wings and all the magic of the occasion that was absorbed when the day began to fade. All at once you will belong to the company of fowlers and talk about your particular gun, your cartridges, your leaking boots, the chilblain on your ear and how to cook a goose.

Oddly enough, the way of cooking fowl is rarely discussed with any confidence. Put a potato in the goose, says one, or a large onion; steep the bird in salt water and give it many cleansings afterwards, says another. A duck is a duck. The man who brings two or three out of his bag hardly cares whether they are served with orange sauce or not. He went off on to the marsh with an apple in his pocket, a lump of cheese and a crust and comfort of any sort, inward or outward, concerns him very little. I would tell you how to cook a goose if I knew the age of your bird. In cold weather it can hardly be kept too long, especially if it is a big greylag, but again it may have been shot from behind and the intestines ruptured which hastens the process of decomposition and makes the meat tender before it has hung so very long. The average fowler is no culinary expert and many of them have never troubled to pluck and dress the teal and would give away their bag if called upon to prepare it for the pot.

In half a lifetime I have made the acquaintance of a great many members of the fowling fraternity, individuals and members of clubs. Among them are one or two whose company on the marsh I have come to appreciate, men who never spoilt their chances, or my own, by doing any of the all too simple things that ruin a flight, looking upwards, moving across the open mud at the wrong time, firing when the general strategy was to allow the first flight to pass. These same individuals are creek-wise and tide-wary, as sure on the mud as a skilled rock-climber on the crags, resourceful and watchful. It takes more than a year or two to learn the ways of fowl, the hazards of the tide, the meaning of all the signs that are there to be read when duck come or go or geese turn and shun a place. You must qualify for this kind of company travelling alone. A hundred people will tell you what you should know, but only time will sift the fact from fiction, time and experience.

The fowlers you meet away from the marsh and the estuary will not necessarily include the men with the widest experience, those in whose footsteps you might follow, but I trust that as you venture you will here and there have the good fortune to meet at least one or two of the old school and take the same path. My own steps on the marsh instilled in me the conviction that nothing a fowler can really enjoy is attained without discomfort, without a degree of risk, a cold and bleak vigil and periodic disappointment and frustration. I knew this long ago when I saw the one-armed man coming uphill to the town one bitter winter's day with a brace of geese slung over his heavy gun. I remember the look on his blue-cheeked, pinched face and the light that was in his eyes as we looked at one another. 'I've got my geese,' he said without speaking. 'I've been out there and crossed the quicksand and come back again while the men of this place are warming their hands at the fire and only mongrel dogs are in the street!' This I heard quite clearly and I remembered it as we jogged home along the frozen road and up the long steep hills on the way. I was not at all put aside when respectable people clicked their tongues and talked about the spit-at-their-boots town-loungers and good-for-nothing fellows who propped the street corners. One day, I said to myself, I would cross the same sands, keep the same vigils, discover the secrets of the flights of duck and geese in the bay. I cannot claim to have acquired as much knowledge as I should, but I know what the flight meant to the one-armed fowler and many more of his kind who go down to the estuary as he did.